Wilderness
Mother

Wilderness Mother

Deanna Kawatski

WHITECAP BOOKS
Vancouver/Toronto

Published by arrangement with Lyons and Burford, Publishers, 31 West 21 Street, New York, New York 10010.

Printed in Canada

Interior design by Laura Joyce Shaw

10 9 8 7 6 5 4 3 2 1

Canadian Cataloguing in Publication Data

Kawatski, Deanna, 1951–
   Wilderness Mother

   ISBN 1-55110-168-8

   1. Kawatski, Deanna, 1951–   2. British Columbia, Northern—
Biography.   I. Title.
FC3845.N67Z49   1994   971.18   C94-910020-X
F1089.N67K39   1994

Contents

For Natalia, Ben,
and the Ningunsaw Valley

Acknowledgments

My thanks move in the following directions:

To Jay Kawatski for leading me into such a unique and wonderful way of life.

To Natalia and Ben for accepting my vanishing act all those mornings when I went to the German cabin to write.

To Richard and Margaret Klocker for their warm hospitality and use of their cabin for that vital week in which I got a solid start on *Wilderness Mother*.

To Pat Grue, Denis D'Amour, Lynne Thunderstorm, Janet Sims, Darrell and Norma Jean Adzich, and Fritz Handel for being true friends and for helping me through one of the most difficult times of my life, which happened to coincide with the writing of this book.

To my sister, Donna Trent; her husband, Rick; and my mother, Lorna Barnhardt, for helping my children and me resettle in the midst of this project.

To E. J. Miller-Towle for her ongoing encouragement and support, and for making me the charm to hang above my desk.

To Joy Krenz for her wise words and belief in my book.

To Peter Fossel at *Country Journal* for publishing my article, which caught the attention of Peter Burford.

To my publisher, Peter Burford, for giving me this opportunity to share some of my wilderness experiences.

To my editor, Lilly Golden, for her insights, helpful advice, encouragement, and support.

To all the wild creatures—both plant and animal—of the Ningunsaw Valley, who enriched my years there and whose presence breathes among these pages.

Above all, thank you to the divine powers of the universe through which all things are possible.

Chapter 1

Mountaintop Meeting

"LET'S GET OUT of this godforsaken place," one ranger hollered to the other. The two men bounded off down the alpine slope, leaving me more alone than I had ever been.

It was June 1978, and I was the first female lookout attendant ever to be stationed at the Bob Quinn Lake fire tower. Ironically, I had chosen this solitary station in a remote corner of northwestern British Columbia at a time in my life when I craved nothing more than a mate, a home, and children of my own. I was twenty-eight.

I closed the collar of my down vest against a fresh blast of wind and surveyed my surroundings. The flimsy shack that was to be home for the next three months sat on a mossy rock at 4,319 feet, just above the tangle of alpine fir at the treeline. A ridge tailed away from me for six miles, gradually climbing upward, its folds embracing snow patches like fallen clouds. All around me was wilderness. The jagged snow-mottled mountains of the Coast Range stood on three sides, while far below the forests were strewn with lakes, like pieces of a puzzle. The Iskut River flowed the full length of the hundred-mile stretch of valley and then was squeezed from sight through a narrow canyon, plunging onward toward its meeting with the mighty Stikine River. To the north stretched the Iskut burn, a gray one-hundred-thousand-acre monster. The unpaved Stewart-Cassiar Highway threaded its way through the silver snags of dead trees that had stood for twenty years. To the west the mountains were still held in the clutches of the last Ice Age. Vast glaciers, rivers of ice, glinted and flowed ninety miles to the Alaska panhandle. Beyond that lay the Pacific Ocean.

This was a land that had never been dominated by the human species. Even the natives chose areas further north and south where the rivers ran red with salmon. For thousands of years these boreal forests had been home to moose, wolves, black bears, grizzlies, lynx, and more. Ravens reeled above the timbered valley bottoms, and wild goats wandered on heights too steep to hold snow.

Amidst the grandeur I contemplated my isolation. What disturbed me most were stories I had heard while stationed in Stewart, 120 miles to the south. It was said that a hermit lived near the Bob Quinn Lake fire tower. His bare feet would inevitably beat a path to my door, the folks warned. They described him as an unpredictable barbarian. Having nothing to defend myself with but a buck knife, I thought warily about receiving an unwelcome visitor. Clearly I was not *that* desperate for male company. I had enough solitary pursuits to keep me busy. And I was tickled by the prospect of making $1,500 a month for doing largely what I wanted.

All my life I had felt most at home surrounded by nature. My twin sister Donna and I were born at Shuswap Lake in Salmon Arm, British Columbia, in 1951. We would have gone on living there year-round, as had three generations before us, if my father had not drowned in 1954, making it necessary for our family to move to the nearest city of Kamloops. After graduating from high school I attended the University of British Columbia, but an acute case of wanderlust cut my academic career short and I headed for Europe. I spent three years abroad.

After I returned to Canada from a trip to Israel and Italy, a friend who had manned Bob Quinn lookout the year before suggested that I apply for the job. I was accepted and in early June found myself flying north in a forestry helicopter with my gear and my new black and white husky pup, Digadee. And here I was.

My accommodations consisted of a single room surrounded by twenty-three windows. The cot, cupboards, table, oil stove, and fridge were all at crouch level so as not to obstruct the view of the fire finder—a heavy platform with a map and a revolving scope—which sat in the center of the room. Heavy cables from the outside corners secured the shack—and none too convincingly—to the mountain.

During the day I would often stare south at Bob Quinn Lake, where a Department of Highways maintenance camp was located but not visible from my lookout. I later learned that it was manned by an ongoing series of transient workers who often came for the isolation and left because of it. Then my attention would rest on Desiré Lake, one and a half miles south of Bob Quinn. Here, rumor had it, the hermit lived in a hand-hewn octagonal cabin.

There was nearly perpetual daylight at this latitude. Each clear night I would watch the sun being swallowed by the jagged peaks. Even at 2 a.m. I would wake up and go outside, amazed to see Venus, the dippers, and Orion hanging in a pale blue sky. Uncannily, each morning I would wake up to the exotic sound of Oriental music wafting out of my single sideband radio that picked up signals from China. No wonder one of my unfortunate predecessors had developed delusions about foreign invasions!

A near constant wind held the bugs at bay. The shack shuddered from its power, and inside the linoleum floor lifted from blasts that exceeded forty-five miles per hour.

At times the entire landscape vanished as the building was wrapped in a cocoon of mist. It was on an afternoon such as this, in late June, as I sat at my table writing, that I saw two human figures emerge from the fog. After nearly three weeks alone I felt vulnerable and self-conscious. There I was clad in a baggy sweat suit, down vest, and clogs. I was relieved to see that my visitors were youngsters. I opened the door and invited inside what turned out to be two young boys on a hike from the Department of Highways camp. Shyly they stepped into the hut, mumbling something about "the others." A moment later two older boys materialized out of the mist, as well as a sleek black Lab and a nanny goat. At the end of the procession came the legendary hermit.

After all the wild stories, I was almost disappointed by how civilized he was. His slim form was clad in a luxurious mink and otter cape over blue jeans and a wool shirt. Possibly for my benefit his blond hair and beard were neatly trimmed and he wore a marten cap on his head. He even wore boots.

He introduced himself as Jay and explained that he had talked the boys from the camp into climbing the mountain with him to spend the night under a nearly full moon. But when a storm almost blasted their tent off the ridge during the night, they decided to seek refuge in the lookout building.

The next morning I asked Jay if he would like to go for water with me. I regularly hauled my water from a distant pond in a fifty-pound jerry can strapped to a Trapper Nelson packboard. With Digadee, Jay's black Lab Penny, and his nanny goat Nahanni at our heels and a cloud of insects enveloping us, we set off down the slope toward the pond. From time to time Jay stooped down to show me miniature ruby cranberries and dwarf blueberries, jewels still on the vines from the previous year. Then he squatted beside a tiny balsam, its wind-sculptured limbs all frozen in the same direction, and told me how trees become stunted at this altitude; this one was at least two hundred years old.

While marmots whistled brightly we wound our way through a vale spilling over with a riot of colorful wildflowers—forget-me-nots, lupins, Alaska harebell, Indian paintbrush, buttercups, monk's hood, and columbine. We picked a lavish bouquet that I took back to the lookout while Jay gallantly packed the water.

Jay left with the others that afternoon and I found myself thinking about him. I was impressed by his energy, knowledge, independence, and powers of observation. I had never met a man whose feet and mouth could move simultaneously at such speed. He had a wonderful laugh and I admired the way he abandoned himself to it. In an age when people were busy examining their personal complexes, he seemed remarkably clear. He appeared to be the freest spirit I had ever encountered.

Five days later Jay returned with some rhubarb wine, homemade huckleberry jelly, and a tiny chair that he had carved from birch. And so our friendship began. Whenever I spotted the red canoe crossing Bob Quinn Lake, far below, I knew that I would see Jay within a matter of hours. In order to visit me he would make a round-trip of nineteen miles. This included fifteen miles of hiking and four miles of paddling. The final trail up the mountain to the lookout was a lung-bursting, near-vertical rise of twenty-five-hundred feet.

Over the course of the summer the "hermit" told me his story. Jay was born in Waukesha, Wisconsin, in 1948 and grew up on a farm. A nature lover from the beginning, he spent his summers barefoot and catching turtles from Pebble Creek, which flowed through the bottom of the pasture. Even then he dreamed of living in the wilderness. At eighteen, on a hitchhiking trip to Alaska, he was captured by the beauty of northern British Columbia and immigrated to Canada.

After a series of desk jobs, Jay, at age twenty-five, made the last payment on his Volkswagen Beetle, loaded it up with enough supplies to last a few months, and headed south of Dease Lake into the stunning Coast Mountains. Hundreds of miles of virgin forests, vast ice fields, and uncharted valleys waited for him.

He spent the next five and a half years living alone in the wilderness. During his first winter he sought refuge in a low, dingy cabin that already existed on the shore of Bob Quinn Lake while he searched the rugged terrain for a building site. He found one that spring on the shore of an unnamed lake later called Desiré.

Jay learned to hunt, to gather and preserve food, and to live in equilibrium with the wild but indifferent land. He was soon able to read whole stories in the cryptic language of animal tracks.

It had been Jay's original intention to live simply by hunting and gathering, but with farming in his background it wasn't long before he was raising chickens and attempting a garden. It soon became apparent that he would never grow a decent garden in the acidic, weed-choked soil near Desiré Lake. Another lengthy search on foot led him to the Ningunsaw River Valley, three miles south of his cabin. There he discovered a natural meadow amid a jungle of spruce, balsam, and cotton-wood. His garden prospered there, and he was rewarded with prime vegetables, largely root crops. These he stored in a root cellar that he constructed in a nearby hillside. Deciding that it would be more sensible to live near his garden, he began building a small cabin on a bench of land overlooking the riverbottom. Now that he had food, shelter, newly acquired skills, and plans for the future, more than anything Jay wanted a woman to share it with.

This was the last place on earth I had ever expected to meet anyone. When Jay came to visit we would bound off across the wind-washed alpine meadows for miles. He was great company, and I caught myself counting the days until his next visit.

I didn't spot a single wisp of smoke that summer. But I did learn that I could survive and even thrive in an isolated setting. At the end of the season I flew back to Stewart by chopper. I had missed a chance to say good-bye to Jay, and at the suggestion of Jeremy, another lookout attendant, I drove back north from Stewart with him and his wife, Cheryl, to make my farewell. We canoed across Bob Quinn Lake and found the trail to Jay's octagonal cabin near Desiré Lake, only to discover a "gone camping" note tacked on his door. I stepped inside to leave a message for him. Sun streamed through a bay window where tiny tea roses grew. Wolf skins hung on homemade furniture. There were birch chairs laced with moose hide, a couch, and a table whose edge was adorned with chip carving. Books, wooden toys, and carvings lined the shelves. The cabin was messy but inspired, and I left most reluctantly, closing the door behind me.

Hours later Cheryl and I were out fishing on Bob Quinn Lake when we heard primitive yodeling. I turned and spotted Jay paddling energetically toward us. It turned out that he had been camping on the far side of the Ningunsaw River when his instincts had told him to get home.

At 1 a.m., by the light of the full moon, with the mist rising from the lake, we all set out once again for Jay's. I rode with Jay, and as we faced each other in his canoe he asked me if I could find beauty like this anywhere else. I had to answer no. On shore our little parade of four people with packs, a goat, three dogs, and a cat wound its way along the trail with the aid of one faltering flashlight, tripping over roots, until we finally spied Desiré Lake gleaming in the moonlight ahead of us.

Jay soon had the wood cookstove crackling and was serving us a feast from his cellar, which held a bright array of jars containing peas, pickled tomatoes, huckleberries, jams, jellies, and moose. At 3 a.m. the two of us went for a moonlight swim.

The next morning, before heading back to Stewart, the four of us rattled our way north to the Iskut burn to pick huckleberries. I knelt in the vast patch of crimson bushes with Jay, harvesting what I knew was his main winter fruit. The great lonely wilderness sprawled away from us in every direction. I suddenly realized that I could be happy in such a life.

I returned to my home at Shuswap Lake, and Jay and I corresponded throughout the winter. His letters spoke alluringly of the life that we could share in the wilderness.

Nearly one year later, in June 1979, I resumed my position as lookout attendant at the Bob Quinn fire tower, and when Jay climbed the mountain to visit he presented me with a moose antler engagement ring.

I was very close with my family, and though they were anxious to see me settled, they knew that I would never lead what they considered an ordinary existence. The only doubt my mother expressed after meeting him was whether a completely self-reliant person like Jay had room for me in his life. I had my own doubts as well. I found his boundless energy exhausting and cautiously noted his self-absorption, but I assumed that the latter could be attributed to his years of isolation. Above all, I knew that this was a chance to live a wonderful dream with a man who had become a fascinating friend.

On October 19, 1979, we were married on the shore of Shuswap Lake, beneath a luminous sky, while a small cluster of friends, family, and autumnal leaves shivered behind us. Realizing how little we would see of each other in the future, Donna and I cried as we hugged after the ceremony.

Shortly afterwards, Jay and I boarded the train, weighed down with four suitcases, a full-length mirror, a twenty-pound pail of honey, my skis, and sixteen boxes of assorted belongings. Before me lay a thousand-mile journey and some of my richest years as a pioneering mother in the pristine Ningunsaw Valley.

Chapter 2

Bush Pregnancy and Birth

T HE AIR ECHOED with the yodel of a loon as we stepped into the overloaded canoe and glided across Bob Quinn Lake toward my new home. As sure as the mountainsides showed autumn cranberry beneath the snow, I bore the blush of the earliest stages of pregnancy. Although my condition hadn't been confirmed by a doctor, I was certain of it. Weeks later, when Jay hitchhiked 120 miles to the Stewart hospital with a sample of my urine in his backpack, we weren't at all surprised when the result was positive.

As I clutched the paddle that Jay had made and drove the water back with as much strength as I could muster, I sensed the doors to other possible futures closing. I knew that my new life would permit me to sink roots into a wilderness that was both forbidding and enchanting. And rather than suffering insecurities about being out of reach of a doctor, I welcomed the prospect of being divorced from the stresses of urban existence and immersed in the natural world at such a special time.

Reaching the far shore, we unloaded the canoe, stored our goods in a nearby abandoned trapper's cabin, then flipped the boat upside down beneath a canopy of alder. Donning heavy packs, we set off down the root-twisted trail to Desiré Lake, one and a half miles south. I breathed in the sweetness of pine needles while autumn's last leaves twirled golden around us. I felt happier and more secure than I had in years.

The house in the Ningunsaw Valley was a bare beginning then, and we intended to live in the octagon until our permanent home was habitable. Like any woman pregnant for the first time, I did my share of navel-gazing. I could have happily spent my time sitting on the shore switching my focus back and forth between the changes happening within my own body and the fascinating moods of Desiré Lake.

But within a few days I realized just how much drudgery was involved in a bush existence. Chores such as splitting and packing wood, cooking, and laundry could easily consume whole days if you let them. We had no running water, and the trip back from the clear creek, 250 feet away, with a five-gallon bucket in each hand, was a grueling one. The buckets seemed taller than me; wrestling them back to the cabin, I invariably arrived on the doorstep with wet jeans.

For washing clothes, Jay had built a pair of adjoining wooden tubs, and I used a plunger with a wooden handle and aluminum base to agitate the wash. Other implements included a scrub board and a hand wringer. It was far more pleasant to load the laundry onto the makeshift raft, pole it far out onto the lake, and freeze my fingers scrubbing beneath the lonely cry of an osprey, while a wind from the southwest gradually nudged me back to shore. The thought of hand-washing diapers in the near future didn't thrill me.

Still my thoughts revolved largely around the nicer aspects of approaching motherhood. Since we both wanted our child to have the best possible beginning, my nutrition was of great concern. And as it was our intention to live off of local foods as much as possible, Jay was anxious to get a moose. We were down to the last jars of bear meat and were hoping for snow to make tracking and packing the moose easier. The surrounding woods were now permeated with a presnow silence. Everything—wolves and ravens, even pine trees—seemed to be holding its breath, waiting for the transformation of winter.

I soon learned the full value of light as the days shrunk, like a rapidly closing eye, to five-and-a-half-hour interludes in a world of night. I was no stranger to gas lamps and could still remember the stench of burning hair from when I leaned too close to them as a child at Shuswap Lake. Even so, I felt handicapped by the dimness of kerosene lamps. Jay had been functioning beneath their weak beam for six winters and found the light strong enough to rely on a cap brim to eliminate the glare while he read.

I had brought along several books about pregnancy and birth, and the more we read about the prevalence of induced labor and Caesarean deliveries the less we wanted our baby born in a hospital. Ideally I would have liked to have enlisted the help of a midwife, but the practice of midwifery was illegal in British Columbia and the chances of one traveling to our remote corner were nearly nonexistent. Instead we read as much as we could about labor and delivery, and my belly expanded simultaneously with my desire for a home birth. I had little doubt about my own ability to give birth to our child naturally. Yoga and meditation had been part of my routine for nine years, and they had developed my flexibility and ability to relax as well as deepening my breath awareness. Even so, I couldn't control the wild cravings for fresh oranges, cherries, Havarti cheese, and Swiss-mocha coffee that sometimes possessed me.

Our diet lacked protein, and with the ever-present moose in mind, Jay sewed dog harnesses from red and black nylon. It would be the job of the three dogs, Digadee, Penny, and Boomer, to haul the meat home. Jay had gotten Boomer from a friend in Stewart. He was an aging, narrow-rumped husky with a perpetually wagging tail, sky blue eyes, and the markings of a panda bear.

Two days after the first heavy snow of winter we were dogsledding one of the packed trails between Bob Quinn Lake and Desiré Lake when we came across fresh moose tracks. The animal had crossed the trail only a few moments before. We decided that it would be best if I held the dogs while Jay, in freezing snow up to his thighs, made a mile circuit through the bush, fighting his way through snarls of devil's club and alder, over windfalls, and across bogs in hot pursuit of the moose. It was a black and white day in November. The snow and sky merged, and the conifers stood in stark contrast. Shining flakes flickered down in the half-light and tickled the back of my neck as I stood waiting.

The trail ran along the base of a low ridge populated by a blend of conifers, birch, and poplar. In all the silence I wondered if anything breathed among the boughs.

As I set off again, the dogs eager to fly, Digadee broke into a frenzy of barking. From my seat on the sled I saw a bull moose standing very quietly on top of the ridge, sixty feet away. He appeared to be trying hard to look like a tree.

I called for Jay. His face brightened when he spotted the huge brown beast. He grabbed his rifle and bolted up the hill. I was welded in place by a feeling that I had betrayed the moose. Even though I had eaten and enjoyed meat most of my life, I had never seen an animal die for the cause. Two shots rang through the still air, and then Jay shouted for me.

By the time I had clambered up the steep, snowy hill, my toque knocked askew by a branch, the moose was ready to topple. I could see the suffering in its eyes, and my horror and compassion overflowed into loud sobs. The moose fell and its limbs, long and thin as table legs, kept churning sideways in the snow.

Jay had neither the time nor the inclination to console me. Wielding his pocketknife as skillfully as a scalpel, his index finger extended to the tip so that they moved as a single instrument, he sliced the moose near the base of the neck, severing the artery that pumped the blood to the head. The next job was to turn the moose over onto its back.

Grunting and struggling, we managed to maneuver the giant beast that reeked of wounds, sweat, and willow branches. Jay whipped some rope from a pocket and tied the legs to adjacent trees. I felt like a nurse in an operating room as he did all the precision work while I held hooves and fetched more rope from the sled.

Jay quickly cut in a circle around the anus, working meticulously to sever the surrounding muscles without penetrating the intestines. With the rope I handed him he then tied up the anus. Next he enlarged the opening in the neck and, grasping the windpipe and gullet firmly, tied the ends tightly and then sliced them off near the head. Returning to the rear end, he carefully slit the skin along the belly open to the sternum. My nostrils filled with the odors of hot blood, moose dung, and undigested vegetable matter. Kneeling near the scrotal area, again Jay cut through the thin muscle and tissue that contained the body organs, taking pains not to puncture the intestines or the stomach, which was filling up with gas and resembled a gray-veined water balloon.

Hands smeared with blood and black moose hair and with muscles straining, Jay pulled the liver and stomach outward as much as he could without ripping anything. Next he cut the diaphragm loose from the rib cage; then, returning to the neck incision, he passed the rope attached to the windpipe and gullet through the chest from the front and grasped it at the center cavity. He then drew the short rope on the anus through the pelvic arch and up through the center opening. Handing the bloody rope ends to me, my husband explained, "Now pull on these real slowly and steadily while I cut any tissue that's still holding the organs in place." I was startled by how heavy the guts were, but with steady effort we extracted them intact. Soon the liver, kidneys, and heart were lying like giant gems in the snow.

What lay in front of me was life-giving meat. I silently thanked the moose and vowed not to waste a single morsel.

Darkness had descended by the time we were done, and we had little choice but to leave most of the meat where it was until daylight. I went to bed that night praying that the wolves wouldn't find it first. Packs regularly ventured as close as two hundred feet from the cabin door, their chilling choruses wafting through the woods.

The next morning we were relieved to find the meat undisturbed. Jay quartered the moose on the hill, and it was relatively easy to maneuver down the slope and load onto the sled. The dogs, knowing that they'd get a share, were eager to haul it home. We hoisted the four quarters up into a cache beside the lake. Luckily the weather remained cold enough to allow us to eat fresh meat for over two months. The remainder was either smoked or canned. Much was packed raw into jars, while other chunks were roasted lightly and then sliced and packed. We processed the meat in sterilized jars using a pressure cooker. Each jar was put under ten pounds pressure for ninety minutes, and once it was safely sealed it was labeled and stored.

In early March, my sister Donna came to visit and brought enough baby clothes for triplets. I didn't realize how much I missed my family until I saw her and her son, Dorian. Donna was skeptical about my isolated existence and also about my husband; she found him uncompromising and demanding. I stressed to her how much I loved the bush, but also admitted that Jay, even with all his good points, was difficult to live with. I cherished their fleeting presence and was miserable after they left. But I had plenty to prepare for in the coming months.

I still hadn't made a definite decision about having a home birth and, considering the risks involved, the Stewart hospital seemed like the best alternative. Toward the end of March, Jay and I snowshoed the four miles to the highways camp and got a ride into town with the foreman's wife. I wanted a thorough examination and also to find out the local doctor's approach to delivery.

Hours later the doctor admitted, in a cultured British accent, that I was in fine health. But since I was almost twenty-nine he didn't want to take chances with his lack of facilities. If there were any complications during delivery, women had to be flown from Stewart to Terrace, the nearest northern city, a full 250 miles from our bush home! The doctor told me to return in May. I left his office feeling old and conspicuous, since by then I looked like I had a cannonball beneath my shirt. Suddenly I was unsure of myself. I hadn't revealed my wish for a home birth to the doctor. If delivery in the Stewart hospital seemed a risky business to him, I figured I would spare him the heart attack.

On the way home I held onto the bottom of my stomach as we staccatoed for 120 miles across an incredible array of potholes. That evening Jay and I wearily snowshoed back across Bob Quinn Lake. The trip to town and back was exhausting. I had badly swollen ankles at the end of it and my throat was raw with the beginning of an infection.

This was the first ailment I had suffered since becoming pregnant, and it intensified my uncertainty about where to give birth to our baby.

By April, winter was letting go its grip on the land. The snow mounds were subsiding and the woods echoed with the hammering of sapsuckers in search of bugs in the bark of the deciduous trees. As the daylight hours expanded, my optimism about a home birth returned. By May, ribbons of bare earth ran their parallel course along the mountains and the gooseberry leaves had opened to reveal a vivid green.

The ice on the lake had broken into huge crystallized slabs that looked like spun glass. We listened to the music of ice chimes, the wind whipping tunes from its tiny caverns, as we knelt near Bob Quinn Lake and gathered minute egg-shaped leaves from the dwarf shrubs of the kinnikinnick plant. Native women traditionally drank a tea made from them to encourage a fast labor, and I was willing to give it a try. But all it gave me was an acute case of diarrhea.

We had three emergency birth kits packed. One we left at the octagon, one was in the partially built cabin in the valley, and one Jay carried in his pack in case we were surprised on the trail. They each contained blankets, gauze, twine, and toilet tissue. I was healthy and in good spirits but also a little disillusioned by the fact that late spring in the north was heralded by armies of mosquitoes. We sought escape from them, and caught fresh fish at the same time, by poling our crude raft far out onto Desiré Lake. The local osprey soared above us releasing its solitary cry, and we watched it settle itself in the ancient ragged nest that crowned a dead spruce. We were accompanied by toads in many shades of green and brown. They crept between the logs and fastened swollen eyes upon us. Now and then they would hop in and take a swim, but mostly they were content to ride. Their mating season had been in early May and the shoreline was inky black with dime-sized pollywogs. A great long line of them poured, always in a counterclockwise direction, around the lake and then toward the mouth of the creek, moving as a single mind in search of its messiah.

A particular loon couple returned to Desiré Lake each spring, as they would each year for the rest of their lives. As we poled toward a cove on the south end of the lake we watched the splendid birds glide closer and closer. Then the male dipped beneath the surface and swam streamlined alongside the raft, his neck extended and his feet well out behind. Bursting from the water within an arm's reach of us, he bore a startled expression, then flowed back to the side of his waiting mate. Her crimson eyes were fixed upon us as she warned us in her eerie voice to stay away, stay away. The loon's dark head shone green while her black neck band stood out in contrast to the intricate pattern of stripes on her body. We spotted the reason for the loon's distress. Nestled in the tall grass right beside the lake was their nest. As the raft crept closer we saw within it two large olive-green eggs with purplish speckles. Even though loons deftly soar through the water, they can scarcely walk on land and hobble only far enough to make their nests. They never have more than one or two babies—just enough to replace themselves—and often the young don't survive. About to give birth at any moment myself, I sensed the sacredness of this spot and the loon's need to feel secure and unharassed. With the aid of a wind from the southwest we glided back to the cabin and left them in peace.

My due date, June 15, came and went. Jay and I were both restless and I grew moody and depressed, plagued by the usual insecurities about a home birth. What if something went wrong? What if the baby died? Would I be strong enough to shoulder the blame? I could face my own death, but surely the death of my child would be too much to bear. Then I calmed as I reasoned that babies also die in hospitals, that life never comes with guarantees. Intuitively I knew that at home was where our baby was meant to enter the world and that everything would be okay.

It hadn't rained for weeks and we were concerned about our garden in the Ningunsaw Valley. At this crucial stage of pregnancy I didn't want to be on my own while Jay traveled on foot to look after the crops. So on June 18 we trudged together to the valley. Throughout the afternoon and far into the evening we toiled, thinning and weeding, then packing water to the orderly rows of vegetables. Later, outside the unfinished cabin, I wearily prepared us a moose stew on the fire pit that was closed in with an old cast-iron stove top. Famished from the exertion, we eagerly sat down to our simple supper, but as we did so I discovered that my tailbone was extremely tender. I couldn't find a comfortable position to sit in. Even though Jay had maneuvered the best stump over for me to perch on, its stubborn surface caused me greater discomfort than before.

We and several hundred mosquitoes spent a restless night on loose boards in the rough loft. The next day the sun beat down on us as I thinned beets and Jay watered. As my fingers sank into the rich, moist soil I did my best to ignore the stinging insects and tried to revel in the sights and sounds of spring. The baby green leaves of elderberry, alder, poplar, birch, and cottonwood had unfurled to their full glory. Tiny winter wrens with their gigantic songs perched on alder branches while tuxedoed robins skittered across the garden. They joined the chorus of scores of songbirds while a male ruffed grouse, just beyond the clearing, accompanied them with drumming. But more and more I was finding it difficult to move from row to row, and I also felt a strong urge to sleep.

A half hour later Jay and I ventured out to the river to rest and escape the insects, which preferred the woods to the open, wind-swept river flat. As we broke out of the timber we spotted two mountain bluebirds flickering through the alder like tiny pieces of fallen sky. Then we stretched out onto the warm black sand and began to take turns reading aloud from *Great Expectations.* The irony of our choice of book was not lost on me.

Suddenly I was seized with the realization that we had no time to spare. We had to set out for Desiré Lake immediately. I had no wish to give birth in our sketchy home in the valley. It took mere minutes to pack and set out.

The first lung-bursting hill we had to climb was a fifty-degree slope with a rise of two hundred feet. It was like toiling up twenty consecutive flights of stairs. Mosquitoes clung to the undersides of thimbleber-ry leaves, then flew forth in ever-swelling battalions to attack us. Through their ranks wafted the aroma of cottonwood leaves, and I glanced at the mosaic of treetops against an indigo sky. Although even in my state I was accustomed to ten-mile hikes, at the top of the hill my calves ached and my upper body trembled.

After plodding to the summit of the next hundred-foot rise I felt a sudden gush of warm liquid down my legs. The amniotic membrane had burst! It was 5 p.m. and my contractions began instantly. I had two and a half miles of rugged trail yet to go.

Jay put his hand gently on my back. "You can do it," he encouraged, wiping more insect repellent the length of my arms. The insects now surrounded me in screaming masses. After my water broke thousands of bloodthirsty mosquitoes were magnetically drawn to me. It took every ounce of my concentration to focus on my breathing during the contractions as the bugs invaded my eyes, ears, nose, and throat. All I could hear was their sanity-shredding whine.

Jay tried to reassure me. "You have lots of time and energy."

I turned to him. "I'll tell you one thing," I vowed. "There's no damned way I'm going to give birth out here!"

Storms of orange and black butterflies released themselves with every step I took on the path ahead. Flickering by our heads, they competed with the whining mosquitoes for space, chaperoning us through the birch and balsam. I had never seen so many in one place, and their presence gave me fresh hope—a signal of my metamorphosis as a mother.

But the trail remained an obstacle course of windfalls, steep hills, and boot-sucking bogs. Two hours later, filthy and exhausted, we reached the cabin. My wet pants were mud from the knees down and my face and arms were smeared with repellent, sweat, and squished mosquitoes.

I kicked off my gum boots and knelt on the floor, preparing for an-other contraction. Jay flew into activity. He lit the fire, packed and heat-ed water, fed the animals, and threw together a dinner of beet greens, spinach, lettuce, scrambled eggs, and raspberry leaf tea. Between bites, I had to drop to the floor on all fours, the position in which I felt most comfortable and better able to cope with the contractions.

We moved the mattress in front of the bay window facing Desiré Lake and I knelt and concentrated on my breathing. The agony was more than I had anticipated, and I struggled to focus attention on a strong pine tree outside the window, imagining my spine as the trunk.

Meanwhile, Jay kept himself occupied by frantically chopping up three gallons of rhubarb that he had packed from the garden. Each time I gasped, "Here comes another one!" he'd drop the knife and fly over to massage my back with baby oil. My back pain was excruciating. I downed at least two gallons of water, which I sweated out.

The summer solstice was a day away and it was only between midnight and 4 a.m. that Jay needed a flashlight to check my progress. The loon couple swam close to the cabin and continued to call, at regular intervals, all through the night. I did my share of howling, as did the dogs outside the window.

The pains came closer and closer. In desperation to be free of them, I began to push. Glistening with sweat, I begged Jay, "Don't take your hands off the small of my back!" I felt that if he did I would fall into an abyss. Through it all the loons yodeled on, the surrounding woods and mountains echoing with their unearthly laughter.

At 4:30 a.m. Jay checked my dilation for the umpteenth time. "I see a head up there with a lot of long black hair on it!" he yelled. He held a mirror beneath me, and, seeing our baby, I beamed.

Squatting, my face dripping with perspiration, I tried to keep control by panting but I was suddenly seized by such a strong urge that I found myself growling like an animal and pushing. Dawn light was filtering into the cabin and the loons released another wild chorus. Suddenly the infant's head burst through, and with more straining the entire length of body slipped through, with the glossy cord trailing after.

"My baby!" I screamed as Jay fumbled with the wet body. He flipped the baby around to get the twice-wound cord off its neck. The infant was the color of moonstone and the head was so pointed that I wondered what planet it had come from. Raising the baby to his mouth, Jay sucked the mucus out of its nose and mouth and it began to kick and cry. Jay glowed with joy and then burst out laughing. "We don't even know whether we have a boy or a girl!" On closer inspection we discovered that I had been right all along. We had a baby girl. It was 5:20 a.m. Labor had lasted twelve hours.

Feeling at last able to succumb to exhaustion, I lay down for the first time. Jay gently placed the baby on my stomach and I massaged the buttery layer of vernix into her skin. A moment later she amazed us by suddenly hoisting herself up on elbows and knees. Holding her head up, she stared straight into my face, taking a good gander at the outside of the vessel that she had been riding in for so many months.

Jay, with hair tousled and eyes bright and optimistic, sucked more mucus out of her mouth with a piece of indoor watering hose. Seeing that the blood was already clotted in the umbilical cord, Jay tied it off with boiled cotton twine and cut it with sterilized scissors.

Holding our baby close I murmured, "our little Natalia!" It was a name I had become attached to while reading Tolstoy's *War and Peace*. Nat quickly found a breast and began gulping down the rich yellow colostrum.

Instantly in love with this new earthling, I was unconcerned about completing the birth process by delivering the placenta. My world had been transformed, and as she worked away at my breasts like a greedy puppy, the osprey swooped over the cabin, sending forth its ringing cry. Morning sunlight danced upon Desiré Lake, and in the distance the Coast Mountains soared. The struggle was over. The sweat had dried on my body and, even after birth, my baby and I still seemed physically joined.

Jay wasn't as calm as I. As the minutes wore on he became increasingly nervous, knowing that the placenta should be delivered about twenty minutes after the baby. This is often a stage where hemorrhaging occurs. Trying his best to stimulate a reaction, he massaged my belly and breasts. Yet I was so relieved that my daughter was born that I didn't share his anxiety. When Jay told me that nearly three hours had passed I was amazed. To me it seemed mere minutes.

I had delivered Natalia in a squatting position. Reasoning that nothing was going to happen while I was lying on my back, I now resumed this posture. After giving a few more pushes the placenta slithered out intact and resembling a calf's liver. I wrapped Natalia in a sheet and took her to bed for a well-deserved sleep.

Within a day Natalia's misshapen head had straightened out and there was a healthy glow to her cheeks. Her dark hair and face resembled mine. And as far as we could see she was perfectly formed.

The next day when we set the kitchen scale on the wooden table beneath the skylight and weighed her, we learned that Natalia was a healthy seven pounds, twelve ounces. The volume of her crying assured us that she had made a safe crossing from the spirit world to the cabin beside Desiré Lake.

Chapter 3

Bush Life with
an Infant

N ATALIA'S ARRIVAL WAS like a rebirth for me. It transformed my
life and I saw everything as though for the first time. Having em-
barked upon parenthood later in life, I was able to take in stride the
many disruptions to my quiet routine. The warm little creature quickly
established herself as the center of my existence, and I soon came to understand the language of her cries. Each was successfully designed to
gain my attention. One meant "I'm hungry," another, "I'm wet and
cold," and yet another, "I've got gas." Her rasping cry could be heard
far out on the lake where, in the breeze, I bent over the tub and
scrubbed clothes. When Natalia couldn't summon me with this wail,
she would unleash her most desperate heart-tugging plea, breaking
into a delightful coo-cry. I remain convinced that it was loon-inspired.

A week after Nat was born I was strong enough to swim across Desiré Lake and back, the frigid distance of a mile. In the center the loons
joined me and glided alongside, their scarlet eyes regarding me. Every
now and then they dove under, vanishing from sight only to reemerge
on my opposite side.

On the evening of July 8 I sat beside the lake breast-feeding Natalia.
From the beginning I had found this to be a very positive and satisfying
form of feeding for both of us, and it puzzled me why women sometimes
rejected this intrinsic part of motherhood. After all, breast milk is the ul-

timate convenience food! As Natalia gulped down the sweet milk the loons were calling with increasing jubilance, and I wondered what they found so amusing. Then I noticed two rather off-key voices joining in their nightly serenade. Down a path of gold sent forth by the sinking sun, the loon couple ushered two fluffy offspring. A happy family.

Natalia was born into a world dissected by mosquito netting. It covered the top of the basket she slept in, which Jay had made by weaving strands of moosehide across a pine pole framework. I sewed a white canvas liner for her little bed and we padded it with blankets and rabbit fur. Nat would lie there sleeping, like a fairy in a flower, undisturbed by the menacing drone of mosquitoes that constantly encircled her.

I would take Nat on walks through the forest, which glowed with miniature dogwood. She rode in a pack strapped to my front, with a piece of mosquito netting draped over the top. If we were to be riding in the canoe, Jay wore the baby basket over his pack, like a turtle shell. With the basket in the center of the canoe and a cloud of bugs thick enough to slice hovering around, we would hastily transfer her from one cocoon to the other, rapidly squishing any opportunists that had managed to zip in. Once out on the water we would lose our tormentors, and Nat was content to be rocked by the gentle waves. Quickly it became routine for her to howl all the way home across the lake, and then I would remember nostalgically the days when it was only Jay and me and the dipping of our paddles.

The mosquito raids on our child made us more anxious than ever to move to the Ningunsaw Valley, where we'd find relief from the bugs once we had built a solid shelter. The tiny cabin there still lacked floors, windows, and a door.

We spent the next several months moving back and forth between the two places, our mobility hampered by a baby and paraphernalia to pack along. I would set out to hike the three rough miles with Natalia strapped to my front in a corduroy pack. On my back was another knapsack containing diapers, baby powder, Vaseline, spare undershirts and sleeper, rabbit-skin moccasins, rattle, teddy bear, and blanket. Stoically I was sandwiched between Natalia's person and her anticipated demands. Since I was unable to see past my cargo to what my feet were doing on the erratic trail, it was much like being pregnant again.

Between Desiré Lake and the Ningunsaw Valley there were a total of three swamps to negotiate over a hazardous network of slick pieces of log placed as stepping-stones across the wetness. But they could unexpectedly give way under foot and at times, while I clutched Natalia, one leg would get sucked into the swamp to above the top of my gum boot. After wrenching my foot out of the muck while my daughter squawked indignantly, I would park and empty my boot and wring out my sock. Nat was oblivious to everything apart from her own desire to be swaying with the rhythm of my walking. With four pack straps and the force of gravity tugging at my chest, I would ascend the sharp hill that succeeded each swamp like a laboring horse.

Halfway to the Ningunsaw Valley was a rocky knoll topped with gnarled pine. It was often a rest stop where I would plunk down and open my built-in snack bar. While Nat gobbled greedily, I would breathe in the cool breeze and view of the shining Coast Mountains. This brief respite was followed by the most treacherous part of the trail. A gorge was spanned by a crude bridge made several years earlier by the falling of trees from either side. Two trees long, the bridge had rotted or sagged in parts; without good balance, no route was safe. Clumsy footing could result in a plunge to the bottom of the gully twenty-five feet below. I was relieved each time I reached the opposite bank safely. One and a half miles later I finally scrambled to the valley bottom, eager to shed my precious burden—none the worse for wear—and relax, but there was usually work to be done.

Often Jay would leave Natalia and me alone at the octagon and set off on his own to work on the new building. He was extremely independent, and I felt a bit left out because it had been my intention to be involved in all aspects of the development of our home. But for the most part I didn't mind. Life revolved around our daughter's needs, and I didn't believe in denying a new baby anything in the way of breast milk, attention, or love.

The same year that Natalia was born an old friend of Jay's, Joe Langerholc, showed up. He was a miner by trade, and Jay had met him while he was employed by the Granduc Mine north of Stewart. Dressed in denim, his square jaw jutting out from beneath the broad brim of a cowboy hat, Joe told us—in as few words as possible, because he was a man of few words—his plans to move to the bush. Jay showed him a spot only half a mile northeast of our building site in the Ningunsaw. I was upset because I had a dream of building a writer's hut in the same lovely meadow, but Jay's generous spirit sometimes overrode my quiet wishes. Joe built a hut there and toughed it out through the winter, living largely on bannock and beans. When he ran out of kerosene and money, he began to use moose fat for candles, tearing his long underwear into strips for wick. The cabin blackened and so did Joe's enthusiasm. He left the very next spring, before we moved down.

Two months later, in April 1981, when Natalia was almost one year old, we made our permanent move. Our embryonic cabin had developed as quickly as our daughter, and once it had windows and a door it was truly born.

Our main window came from the house that my parents had built together at Shuswap Lake. My sister Donna, her nine-year-old son Dorian, and Donna's friend Gordie had trucked it one thousand miles north for us when they came to visit during my first February. When it reached Bob Quinn Lake safely, the worst of its journey still lay ahead. The next morning, beneath a bright blue sky with feathery clouds etched at random in the southwest, Jay and Gordie trudged back across Bob Quinn Lake to get the window. Penny, Boomer, and Digadee trotted along pulling the white homemade sled with the canvas flaps. Behind it they towed Dorian on skis. His blue eyes twinkled with the excitement of a new experience as he hung onto a red nylon rope attached to the sled and sped across the wind-scoured surface of the snowy ice.

The six-foot by three-foot window, which included two wing windows that opened on each side, had to be propped upright on the narrow sled. With Dorian skiing behind, it was smooth sailing back across Bob Quinn Lake. Donna and I were relieved to see the parade pull to a stop in front of the octagon with the window still intact. Whenever Jay and I discussed house plans my priority was lots of light, and I was most anxious to see this window arrive in the valley in one piece.

The trail between Bob Quinn and Desiré Lake was mainly level, but it rose and dipped at the beginning, and if the dogs got ahead, they could easily speed down a slope too quickly, oblivious to the fate of their prize cargo. To prevent any accidents, Jay and Gordie would have to trot along on either side, controlling the dogs with a rope and steadying the load.

After lunch we all set out for the Ningunsaw Valley. There was no dampening the dogs' enthusiasm, and Jay, Gordie, and the team pushed ahead while I, then six months pregnant, hiked with Donna and Dorian. Despite the tangle of swamps followed by hills, the first serious obstacle proved to be the halfway point. The dog team had to be coaxed and maneuvered down into the gorge and up the other side, while the cargo swayed precariously.

After toiling another one and a half miles, we reached the last two-hundred-foot drop into the valley, which made the rest of the trail look easy. On this final slope, made slick with snow, Jay and Gordie gripped the ropes and did their best to control the team. When they reached the bottom, red-faced and sweat-streaked, and examined their cargo, they discovered only one small crack in the upper left-hand corner of the window to commemorate its journey.

It became our kitchen window, through which I could glance up from my simmering moose stew or rising bread and seek out the forest life and the cool heights of the mountains beyond. The window faced east across a flat bench of land that we gradually turned into a yard. East from the house the yard extended about 150 feet; along its edge, at my request, we left several birch trees. Forty feet below, what we came to call Natty Creek turned a sharp bend, changing its course from south to west, so that our homesite, although at a higher elevation, was bordered on two sides by the meandering of the creek. Natty Creek had two sources. One was a stream that flowed out of Little Bob Quinn Lake, about three miles north of our place, and the other came from Elbow Lake, two miles northeast of us. The two streams ran together at a place on our trail that we called Burl Junction, named for a giant burl growing on a cottonwood tree that stood there. The last mile of our three-mile trail from the house to the Stewart-Cassiar Highway followed south along Natty Creek. The footpath wound mainly through dense timber and took an hour to hike.

Natty Creek finally flowed into the Ningunsaw River about one mile west of us, at the far end of the three-hundred-acre river flat upon which we lived. Many years after we settled in the valley, for the sake of electricity, Jay built an earth-fill dam on the creek, and the resulting pond was visible from the kitchen, as was the wide path that was created as Jay picked away at the southeast corner of the yard for dirt with which to build the dam. In the east on the opposite side of the pond site was a two-hundred-foot-tall tree-lined ridge that blotted out part of the morning sun. My view to the south extended beyond one of the gardens, which lay on the opposite side of Natty Creek and above a wall of giant spruce, balsam, and cottonwood, to the six-thousand-foot-high snowy peaks of the Coast Mountains on the far side of the Ningunsaw River. Even though the river wasn't visible from the window, nor indeed from the clearing, it was a mere five-minute walk through the woods, a distance of a quarter of a mile from our house.

Jay built our door with heavy pine boards, held together with wooden pins. Doorknobs were fashioned from two heart-shaped burls, and at the center of the door he attached a knocker that he had carved in the shape of a fist.

The cabin was built from pine and spruce logs from the surrounding woods. Jay had erected the initial structure alone, before I arrived, and he had looked to the steep hillside above for suitable trees, since they were comparatively easy to maneuver down the slope. Each log was notched the full length, as well as at the corners, then lined with insulation before it was fitted against the one below. From the outside the cabin resembled a Swiss chalet, with a steep-pitched roof made from hand-split balsam shakes, extending nearly to ground level and creating substantial eaves.

Soon after moving to the Ningunsaw Valley we realized that we needed more light in the cabin. On a cloudy day it was far too dim for reading or sewing. When a freak April snowfall smothered our little clearing, making outside work impossible, Jay decided that it was time to make a window on the back side of the house facing the hill. The hole would be cut with a chain saw. He thought it best if he started out working from the inside. I was convinced that such a deafening noise in our tiny space would cause Nat to panic. But my protests fell on ears already encased in protective shells. In minutes the chain saw was obnoxiously chewing through the fat logs at full volume, releasing jets of sawdust and clouds of gasoline fumes. I watched in disbelief as Nat picked up her cookie-tin drum and began to beat it with her rattle, at the same time doing her best to outyell the machine.

Our twelve- by sixteen-foot cabin was built on five different levels. These, rather than walled rooms, defined our living space. I never knew where to put Nat to safeguard her from falls, but the place was simply too small for walls, and we didn't wish to interrupt the flow of heat and light.

Just inside the door was a small entryway, with a window facing east. The log walls were lined with hand-planed shelves upon which sat gallon jars full of provisions. Beneath was a row of wooden pegs for coats and hats. A high step, which we painted with yellow enamel, between the entryway and the kitchen, made it awkward for packing in wood and water. The floor space in the kitchen wasn't more than five feet across, and I sometimes felt as though I was working on a train. At one end was a large spruce burl sink crafted by Jay. It made an ideal baby bath. Close by and opposite the window was the Findlay oval cookstove, and at the south end was an L-shaped counter space complete with sink. Beneath the counter on the left side was a wood box. Above, a row of handsome pine cupboards with wooden latches ran the full width of the cabin. It was another step up into a dwarf living area, so that when Nat and I were on opposite sides of the counter, which also served as a room divider, we were eye to eye. A sheet of aluminum ran beneath the cookstove, up the wall, and onto the next level; this also served as a shelf for pots and pans. To keep Nat away from the back of the stove, Jay cut, planed, and put up pine railings, which provided a place to hang pots and dry clothes. To protect Nat from accidents, he constructed a number of gates and railings. But as essential as these were they also made it more awkward than ever to move around. A climb of ten steps up a wooden staircase, which we painted with red enamel, led to a four-foot-wide landing. Anyone with a height exceeding five and a half feet was guaranteed to bonk his or her head on the beam at the top, which supported the floor of the loft. Double doors, which Jay made by framing glass from wrecked automobiles, opened out from the tiny landing, which soon became Natalia's library, onto a ten- by four-foot sun deck. Two more steps up in the opposite direction led to the eight- by eight-foot sleeping loft. Due to the slope of the roof it was possible to stand up only in the center of it, and the floor was just big enough for a double bed and a small one for Nat. Along the low roofed edges of the loft we crammed our extra clothing.

The cramped quarters soon spawned a plan for an addition. It was to measure twenty-one by thirty-four feet, with an upstairs and attic. We also planned an outhouse, woodshed, and barn, all of which would be built into the south-facing hillside. Most of our windows would face south, overlooking Natty Creek and the garden below.

In spring the outside work kept us out of our tight quarters, and it was easy enough to take Natalia with us. She loved the outdoors as much as I did, and before she could walk her round bottom seemed to have a magnetic affinity for any spot I parked it on. She wouldn't budge.

By the end of May we had cleared a broad patch of ground on the far side of Natty Creek, part of a plan to expand the garden in an easterly direction. Warblers trilled and the smell of coltsfoot wafted across the clearing. In many places, deep green stinging nettles had nosed their way up through the dead grass. Farther out the forest floor was covered with a plush carpet of moss concealing a maze of fallen trees. Higher up grew a profusion of plants, including red elderberry with their antler-like branches and thorny devil's club. Higher still was an abundance of lichen-tasseled alder; beyond it, towering spruce, balsam fir, and mammoth cottonwood made us feel as insignificant as a trio of forest gnomes.

At a friendly bend in the creek, a giant spruce tree grew. I plunked portly Nat on a quilt beneath the tree and then went to work with Jay. With an ax and mattock we hacked out elderberry bushes, wild raspberry canes, and devil's club. Jay's chain saw chewed through the pumpkin-colored flesh of the larger pieces of alder, and we both stacked the remaining brush into huge piles. Later the tree stumps had to be hacked and dug until they were loose enough to be yanked by a cable attached to a chain saw–driven winch.

Every few minutes I'd glance over at Natalia. In quilted overalls, sweater, and wool hat, she looked as plump and healthy as a cherub. She was content to sit for two-hour stretches, bending with grunts to pick up sticks and spruce cones. While she explored the earth within a two-foot radius of her substantial bottom, we started burning the alder brush. As we flung more pieces of brush onto the fires we were blasted with smoke. Soon the flames leaped ever higher, sending off showers of sparks, and our toques and shirts became riddled with small black holes.

Suddenly I sensed that Natalia was in trouble. I whirled around to see, a short distance away, a crumpled face and tears springing out of her eyes. Her short arms were agitating and her howls competed with the chain saw. She had crawled a short way from the quilt where I'd placed her. Rushing over, I saw she had in one chubby fist a clump of stinging nettles. This plant injects poison into the skin upon contact, and the pain can linger for hours or even days afterwards. Natalia's ruddy face was mottled with white bumps. She had given herself a facial with them! With my work glove, I tore the nettles out of her hand and, scooping her up, forced my smoke-cured body up the steep hill to the cabin. Jay shut the chain saw off long enough to find out what had happened, then rushed back to the garden to tend the fires. The sting of nettles is similar to bee venom, so I treated her with a paste of baking soda and water. Her sobs subsided, but my own sense of guilt didn't. I had assumed that Nat would stay put, but in the future I would take less for granted. The rash soon faded, but one saving grace remained. After this early inoculation, in later years Natalia showed little reaction to stinging nettles.

When Nat was an infant it was easy enough to work around her. While she slept I would go behind the cabin and swing a pick or shovel, doing my part to dismantle the huge section of hill that had to be moved before the addition could be erected. As silly as it seemed to excavate more space in the middle of a vast wilderness, it actually made sense to have the north wall of the cabin snug into the earth. It would be ideal for heat conservation. I enjoyed the vigorous exercise and the brief interludes from the demands of motherhood.

Once Natalia was walking there was no more parking her on quilts for long spells. Whatever we were doing she wanted to do as well. Even after she was weaned from breast-feeding, toilet trained, walking, and talking, we were still toiling with picks, shovels, and an awkward home-made wheelbarrow to remove the loosened dirt. Nat was bright, pudgy, and as strong as a little goat. She was eager to participate in the hill-gouging operation, and Jay attached a short wooden handle onto a pickhead for her. In her red-hooded coat she looked like one of the seven dwarves as she bent and attacked the dirt. Wherever I struck the almond roca-like soil, Nat was always a short distance away at knee level. Her presence prevented me from taking wild swings in case I loosened a rock and sent it hurling down upon her. Every move had to be calculated, and in that way I learned to work mindfully and to cherish all the more this elf with the giant will to help.

The hillside was embedded with rocks ranging in size from pebbles to boulders. The boulders had to be unearthed and put elsewhere. First ensuring that Natalia was a safe distance away, I assisted while Jay, with shovel, poles, and ingenuity, toppled mammoth rocks into predug graves that would form the foundation of our addition.

In wool pants, heavy hand-me-down boots, ear protectors, and cast-off hard hat, Jay felled trees for the new wing. As I held a wide-eyed Natalia tight, the spruce trees, a few of which exceeded two hundred feet, thundered to earth. Nat's face was tense at these times, likely reflecting the concern that I felt for Jay's safety. Felling trees was an extremely dangerous undertaking, and I knew that if he were ever injured I wouldn't be able to haul him out. He would have had to stay alone while I put our twenty-six-pound daughter on my back and ran five miles to the highways camp in hope of retrieving help. Few of the logs for the addition were less than twelve inches in diameter. All had to be moved using a hand-powered come-along—a block and lever device made to move heavy objects—a block and tackle, peaveys, and a chain saw–driven winch.

Before the logs were raised, round by round, they had to be peeled. Dressed in pitch-caked overalls and armed with drawknives, Jay and I straddled the trees and stripped off the coarse bark with long, back-stretching strokes. While the sweet smell filled our nostrils, spruce and pine scales in shades of brown, gray, yellow, and ochre sprayed our faces and spattered the moss-covered ground. Toiling at the task until our stomach muscles ached, we reaped the reward of descending to the smooth pale cambium layer, which glistened with sap. Later in the season, when the bark had loosened, we could peel the trees like giant, somewhat stubborn, bananas. Our daughter would beg for her turn, and dressed in a worn-out set of rain gear to protect her from the pitch, she'd attack the bark with passion. The seriousness with which she took the endeavor was spelled out by her converging eyebrows. Even when red squirrels scampered up and down the standing trees, scolding us incessantly, Nat kept her large eyes on the task at hand. Sometimes I would have to tell her that it would be easier if she held the tool right-side up. The double-handled tool was wider than she was, and with the force she applied to the task, I was relieved that it wasn't any sharper. When I gently reminded her for the tenth time that it was my turn now and took the drawknife from her, she burst into indignant sobs, unable to understand why her help wasn't as valuable as anyone else's. What she lacked in strength and size she made up for in spirit. Jay finally remedied the situation by buying another drawknife at the department store in Stewart so that Nat could have her own.

Gradually our house grew, and Natalia did too. At three years old she could hike ten miles in a few hours and was also showing signs of having a sharp, intelligent mind. Isolated as we were, Nat lacked regular playmates, so I tried to compensate for it by being her buddy. A stump on the hill above the house was our stage for games of charades, and the Ningunsaw River flat was our playground. Often I sang as Nat pranced ahead of me through the woods, then raced down the bank to the expanses of black sand and water-rounded rocks. Together we'd dance, play hopscotch and tag, and build sand castles and stone villages. When my time was consumed by chores, Nat was by my side chopping up onions, helping me bring kindling into the house, and fetching vegetables from the garden. She was also able to entertain herself for hours at a stretch and was old beyond her years, as children who grow up in an adult world often are. Sometimes when she was "reading" or drawing and her parents disturbed her one too many times, she would blurt out, "Don't bother me! I'm toncentating!"

By 1984 the new wing was closed in. With his chain saw, Jay cut the back wall out of the original cabin, creating a broad entrance. Even though the addition was not yet finished on the inside I reveled in this new expanse of living space. The door at the south end opened out onto a front porch, a favorite spot for enjoying the evening view. Beneath the porch was a steep forty-foot drop that leveled off into the grassy, wildflower-strewn banks of Natty Creek flowing the full length of the clearing. Directly below the house was a ten-foot rock face. Jay soon realized that we could use the rock face to our advantage. The climate made it difficult to grow frost-tender crops to maturity, and we both concluded that a greenhouse could solve this problem. We used an area about ten feet wide and twenty feet high, directly below the front porch, and enclosed it in a plastic-covered wooden framework, which Jay attached to the perimeters of the porch. The rock face absorbed heat and provided a support for climbing cucumber vines. An added bonus was that hot air produced in the greenhouse could be channeled up into the house. The only drawback was that the winters took their toll on the plastic and it had to be replaced nearly every year.

The clearing on which we lived was about five acres, and over half of that was visible from the front porch. To the west, a precarious log ramp followed the hillside for forty feet to the outhouse. This small structure, built out of sheer necessity the first spring, was constructed largely from slabs left over from the boards that Jay made with his chain saw attachment. The two-seater faced south, and a broad glassless window offered a clear view of Natty Creek and the garden beyond. One day through this window I watched two otters gleefully bobbing their way down the stream. The outhouse, erected on a steep incline, was designed to be a composting toilet; therefore it wasn't necessary to dig a hole. Some of the largest gooseberries on our clearing grew at its base.

Fifteen steps further west at the bottom of the hill we began our first barn. The logs we used for it were massive spruce that were felled and peeled beside the building site. As the barn grew, round by round, with the help of a peavey, the mammoth logs had to be rolled up pairs of smaller logs running from the ground to the top of the structure. I helped by blocking the brutes to prevent them from rolling back down. I found it unnerving to place small wedges of wood between the log and the supporting poles, praying that they would be enough to keep the logs from tumbling down. Jay never flinched from any task, no matter how formidable, and he looked with scorn at what he considered to be my cowardice. The barn was situated so that the hillside would form the back wall. Jay intended to raise an extensive roof, thereby creating a spacious hayloft, but instead the work on the barn ceased after five rounds. It was closed in with tarps and plastic, and we housed domestic rabbits in cages along the south wall.

On the far western side of the clearing was the original garden, flanked to the south and west by dense forest and to the north by hillside. Closer toward the house, on the north side of Natty Creek, grew three hundred-foot rows of strawberries. Beyond was more garden, which we later turned into a clover patch for the rabbits' food. Much of the original acre of garden was eventually given over to this purpose as well.

A good wood supply was essential to our life-style, and on the opposite side of the house, directly in front of the root cellar, Jay built a sturdy woodshed. Jay labored long hours to erect the solid beams that formed the framework of the new building. He planned it so that there would be a large attic storage space beneath the solid balsam shake roof, and in a matter of weeks it was completed.

By then a crude bridge gave us easier access to the plots on the south side of the creek. From the porch the most prominent features on the far side of Natty Creek were two massive spruce trees on the north edge of the tilled expanse. On the eastern end was the stumphouse, a playhouse Jay made by hollowing out a giant spruce stump and outfitting it with a shake roof and hinged door. A three-hundred-foot row of raspberries ran the full length of this garden, then came to a stop near a bend in Natty Creek. South beyond the garden was a profusion of wild brush, including an abundance of wild raspberries, which we harvested regularly. Beyond them rose emerald virgin forest, with the Coast Mountains glowing beyond.

Natalia was four years old by the time the addition was closed in. I didn't feel right having only one child in our remote setting. Having grown up as a twin, I knew well the pleasure of having another child with whom to share life's experiences. When I asked Nat how she would like to have a brother or sister, she considered the question intently for a moment, then replied, "I'd like to have a sister. I don't know about a brother." Since I didn't wish to bear children beyond the age of thirty-five and I was thirty-three already, I knew that time was running out.

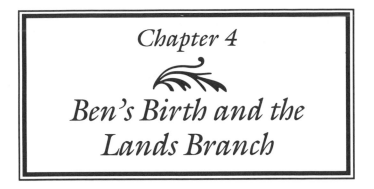

Chapter 4

Ben's Birth and the Lands Branch

IT WAS A bright day in late May 1985. I was three months pregnant and weeding the strawberries when Jay arrived home from Stewart with a certified letter from the Ministry of Lands, Parks and Housing. Wild violets were blooming beside the creek where Natalia, age five, baby-sat ten goslings. Imprinted on her, they followed her everywhere, a peeping parade led by our little barefoot goose girl in a long printed dress and waist-length hair that had turned blond. We both looked up as Jay cheerfully waved the letter in the air and called, "We got our eviction notice!"

Taking the letter from him, I read the official jargon and felt my throat start to tighten. The letter had come complete with copies of sections 57, 58, and 63 of the Land Act, which outlined what steps the government would take in the case of trespass. We were ordered to: *Cease unauthorized occupation, vacate the area, remove any improvements, and leave the Crown land in a safe, clean, and sanitary condition within sixty days of the notice, or the improvements in trespass together with any logs, machinery, equipment, goods, chattels, or other materials would be seized on behalf of the Crown without further notice.* If squatters would not or could not pay for the cost of this removal, their belongings would be sold at a public auction with the proceeds from this event going to the Crown or government in power. I was shocked to learn that on top of all this we could be fined and sent to jail! To make matters worse, the letter had been sitting in the Stewart post office for a month. They wanted us off the property by June 19, less than a month away and the day before Nat's fifth birthday.

It had all begun in 1980, when stories about squatters in British Columbia and the Yukon being burned out by the government had left me feeling very insecure. Homesteading rights no longer existed in British Columbia, and it was next to impossible for the public to acquire Crown land. Because we had chosen to pioneer in the wilderness without waiting a precious lifetime for government approval, we were, in effect, outlaws. I had suggested that we apply for an agricultural lease. If Jay had remained a hermit he would have been content to continue living in defiance of the law, using the notices that came every six months to paper the outhouse, but he was sensitive to my concerns.

Natalia was a newborn infant when we followed the rules and submitted an extensive plan of development for an agricultural lease. A year later we received a formal reply stating that someone would be out to inspect. We saw neither hide nor hair of any Lands Branch officials until 1982. That year Jay was employed as a sediment sampler for B.C. Hydro, which was doing preliminary studies for dams on the Iskut River. A helicopter pilot arrived daily to fly him on a hundred-mile circuit. So certain was Jay that we would be granted some kind of lease once they saw the crops that we grew in a region that wasn't even classed as agricultural, that he arranged to have representatives from the Lands Branch flown in.

Natty watched while the noisy helicopter landed beside the prosperous garden. Two officials emerged and, after a brief tour of the vegetable patch, toiled up the steep bank to the house. Arriving panting in the yard, they were abruptly stopped in their tracks by the sight of our quaint and sturdy log home. One uttered, "It looks like you're planning on being here for a while!"

Inside over tea and cookies at our tiny, hand-built table, the regional director advised us, "It is my duty to inform you that at present you are living in a state of trespass." Nat blinked her big eyes at him and slid another oatmeal cookie from the plate. Jay, who had been cutting boards, smelled like the sawdust that clung to his hair, beard, and clothes.

His eyes flashed, "It was two years ago now that I submitted my plan of development for an agricultural lease!"

The regional director replied tersely, "I'm afraid that an agricultural lease is out of the question until you have road access."

Jay groaned. "That would cost a half million dollars, more than I'll ever have in a lifetime. To be honest, I don't want a road either!"

For the officials, the main concern was legalizing our presence. The only option available to us in our circumstances, and at our economic level, was something called a license of occupation. It was unlike a lease in that we wouldn't be able to own the land, but it allowed us legal tenure, and we would be charged taxes. A few moments later, promising to send the pertinent documents and clutching their policies, the two officials flew away.

We didn't hear another word until 1984. When the letter arrived, we were subsisting on an annual income of $3,000, and the demand for $2,300 within sixty days after months of silence came as a shock. Prosecution for trespass was the grim alternative to paying the fee, which included five years' back rent. We would be charged $200 annually, which was very reasonable, except that it was subject to increase without notice, "at the Crown's discretion." In addition, if the ministry, at any time, deemed our presence undesirable, it could give us thirty days' notice to vacate the property. To top it off, we had been allotted only five acres of "rental space" when there were hundreds of miles of uninterrupted wilderness around us! In essence, the contract gave us few rights but imposed a heap of obligations.

I took up my pen right away and wrote a passionate plea to the regional director. A month later we received a reply. Although he didn't directly respond to any of my statements, he had dropped the fee to $1,053.23, making it clear that this was the minimum cost that the ministry would consider.

Still, we didn't have the money and we withdrew into silence. We were determined to stay in our home. It seemed ridiculous that in Canada, the second largest country in the world, 95 percent of the population clung to a strip stretching a mere sixty-five miles north of the American border. It was understandable that the authorities didn't want people to set out into the bush and build a place on a whim, only to decide a year later that they couldn't tolerate the hardships. The wilderness would soon be littered with tumbledown shacks and garbage. However, a system was needed that would make it possible for the more serious to pursue this path.

The letter we received in 1985—our eviction notice—broke the silence in a brutal way. With our second child on the way, our need for a secure home was greater than ever, and we had already put years of back-breaking work into our place. We had neither asked for nor received any assistance from the government. With so little time left, we decided that it would be best if Jay went to Smithers, a town 250 miles southwest of our homestead, to meet with the regional director. I was anxious to accompany him and offer my support, but someone had to stay home and tend the livestock. Instead, Jay took Natalia and a tape recorder so that I could hear the exchange later. Nat was very worried about the "Yands Branch" and thought that they were going to "shoot Papa."

The government was unaccustomed to negotiating with squatters, and I understood how reluctant the authorities were to set a precedent by granting us any kind of legal tenure. Anxiety weighed heavily upon me, and it was with great relief that I watched my family return home three days later. Via the tape I heard Jay point out a number of the problems with the contract, including that, with the boundaries drawn by the government, we'd be in a state of trespass every time we went to the outhouse! Nat had also spoken up at the meeting, complaining, "Yet's go, Papa. This is boring!"

Luckily, the regional director had been willing to draw up a new contract that was more in our favor. However, it was still only a license of occupation, and even though the director had said that it might be upgraded to a lease in the future, we were still dissatisfied with it. In fact, it wasn't until a cloudy afternoon in August that we searched for a pen and reluctantly signed the contract. Jay took it and the hard-earned $300 (in response to our pleas, The Lands Branch had dropped the fee to this figure) to Stewart to mail. As usual, several weeks elapsed before we heard anything at all.

Meanwhile, Natalia watched with profound interest as my belly grew and grew. As it became harder for her to balance on what remained of my lap, she was distressed to realize that something large and significant was interfering with the closeness that she and I had always shared. The baby, who I was certain was a boy and was already calling Ben, was quite a bit larger than Nat had been, and my instincts told me that I had best go to Stewart so that he could be delivered by a doctor. I had seen a physician only once during this pregnancy.

Finally, in late September, the license of occupation contract was returned signed and sealed. It was good for five years and renewable. For $200 annually we had secure tenure, a house, fertile soil, and much freedom. As autumn spun its gold and the highbush cranberries glowed from the bushes, I experienced a new feeling of peace.

Against the back wall of our addition, Jay was constructing an eight-foot-high and sixteen-foot-long retaining wall out of rocks and mortar, which kept the hillside out of our living room and stored the heat produced by a barrel stove built into its base. The rocks and sand for the project were hauled in from the river, and the ninety-pound bags of cement were freighted up from Terrace and backpacked the last three miles. With steadfast determination, Jay would arrive in the yard nearly bent double from the weight of his load. Although much of the floor remained dirt for a couple of years, in front of the retaining wall was a dropped floor of flat rocks gathered at the river.

Lining the front of the addition, large windows looked east, south, and west. Even one of the smallest was composed of sixteen twelve-inch square panes of glass for which Jay, with great skill and effort, built wooden frames. He set up his workshop beneath these windows, at a level two feet lower than the main living area. Soon, much to my dismay, the walls were cluttered with tools. From one log beam of the high ceiling swung his life-sized carving of an eagle in flight.

Upstairs was another twenty-one- by thirty-four-foot space. After living in close quarters for five years, I was reluctant to see walls being raised. Natalia's corner was toward the north end, while Jay's and my bedroom occupied the south side. There a yellow-paned window, identical to the kitchen window, captured the heights of South Mountain, so named because it lay directly south of our place on the far side of the Ningunsaw River. Above the upper floor an attic ran the full length of the addition.

At the base of the stairs in the back corner sat shelves for storing the food we canned. On top, three substantial blue plastic barrels, which served as storage tanks for our water system, were located. In 1981 a gasoline pump had eliminated the tedious and exhausting chore of hauling five-gallon buckets up a steep forty-foot slope. We ran lengths of black plastic hose from the pump beside the creek to the barrels, which had to be filled about twice a week or more, depending on how much laundry and canning I was doing. Another line went under the kitchen floor to the taps. For the first few years we took our weekly baths in a small round tub. Then with great pleasure we installed a large and luxurious cast-iron bathtub. A wedding present from a trapper friend, this had been flown in by helicopter in 1982. Laundry tubs were situated beside the north door of the addition. Water was heated on the stove in huge kettles and lugged, steaming, to these two locations. This task became more difficult as my belly grew.

Near the end of October, my good friend Pat Grue drove out from Stewart. Jay had introduced me to Pat and Brian Grue when I first moved to the north, and one of the highlights of my trips to town was to visit Pat, who, over the years, had become a vital person in my life. Although my calculated due date was November 12, I thought that the baby would be born around Halloween, and Nat and I cheerfully packed and set out for town with Pat. Jay had to stay home to look after the animals and, in the event of cold weather, to keep the fires going so that the canning didn't freeze. I knew that it would be difficult to get word to Jay so that he could be present for the birth. But I hoped that I would be able to drop a message with someone going by the highways camp, and then one of the road crew could hike down.

Pat was a reluctant driver, and it had taken a good deal of courage for her to drive the Stewart-Cassiar Highway. A slippery layer of ice and snow coated the pothole-riddled road. Halfway to town we had to steer around an Arrow Transport truck, which was jackknifed across the highway. In Bear Pass, an active avalanche zone, it was snowing heavily, and when we finally arrived in Stewart we heard of numerous accidents and were relieved that we had made it safely.

In Stewart, Nat and I passed the time pleasantly enough, and I considered us fortunate to have good friends to stay with. I was happy to have Pat's warm female friendship, and Nat had the companionship of her son, Waylon, who was only six months older than Nat. Even though I expected to give birth within a week or two, I was anxious to make the best use of our time in town. I enrolled Nat in kindergarten to give her a chance to interact with a group of children her own age, and she loved it. Nat would be the first one up every morning, yanking on her navy tights and one of the three dresses she had brought. I did volunteer work at the school, helping groups of slow readers. Sometimes I would see my daughter filing by in a line of children bound for the library or gymnasium. Her honey hair flowed to her waist in waves and her eyes shone with excitement. The younger students were fascinated by my huge belly, and as they passed their reverent whispers would waft up to my level: "She's preeeeegnant!" and "She's gonna have a baaabeee!"

However, when November 12 came and went uneventfully, I grew distressed. Then the north wind started howling savagely and the temperature took a mad plunge to minus 13°F—unusually frigid for Stewart—where it would remain for weeks. I knew that the thermometer in the Ningunsaw Valley would be reading ten or twenty degrees colder and that if it didn't warm up Jay wouldn't be able to leave the place without risk of losing animals, canned goods, and house plants. I contemplated hitchhiking home and walking in to let him know that I hadn't had the baby yet. But what if I went into labor along the way? I felt as if an immense wall of cold was separating me from Jay and I missed him terribly.

Dr. Neilson, the latest in an ongoing series of physicians who rotated through the Stewart hospital, insisted that I visit him a couple of times a week. After I'd been in Stewart for three weeks, just to be on the safe side, he decided that I should go out to Terrace for an ultrasound. Insisting that he needed a break from small-town isolation, Dr. Neilson drove me all the way out and back, a round-trip that took eight hours.

At Mills Memorial Hospital in Terrace, the ultrasound indicated that everything was normal. Next I was sent to an obstetrician who strapped a light to his head like a miner going underground. He was so impersonal that I felt like a frog about to be dissected. I experienced discomfort as he reached in with a glove-encased hand and "stripped the membrane." He then assured me that my baby would be born within three or four days. At the time I was relieved by this news. Two weeks later when I still hadn't given birth, I was at my wit's end and was beginning to wonder if our baby was ever going to emerge into the light of day.

At the end of November, a full five weeks after Natalia and I had arrived in town, Dr. Neilson's term of employment in Stewart came to a close. Soon a new doctor would come to take his place. The night before departing, Dr. Neilson had a nurse telephone to tell me that at the first sign of labor I should come down. I slept soundly, and after waiting until mid-morning on December 1, Dr. Neilson drove out of town. It was a brilliantly sunny Sunday, and an hour later at 11:30 a.m., as I walked beside the Portland Canal with Karen Boissoneault, a friend I had met when I took her aerobics class on one of my visits to Stewart and who was also due to give birth any day, I went into heavy labor. Rushing back to her house, where we had spent so many hours sharing philosophies and child-raising strategies, Karen hastily drove me back to the Grues', where Pat helped me throw some belongings together. Phoning the hospital, she spoke to the only person on duty, a male nurse named Phil. Phil had seen births but had never assisted with one. The other nurses had teased him that he would be the only one on duty when I went into labor, and he would have to handle it all on his own.

When Pat and I bustled in, the thin, bespectacled nurse looked as if his worst nightmare had just come true. His face turned ashen. He stammered, "This is most unfortunate. There is no doctor present." It was the only six-hour lapse when there would be no doctor in town.

My contractions were so close by then that I immediately wanted to squat down on the floor of the delivery room in order to handle them. Ignoring Phil, who protested that it wasn't "standard procedure," Pat took a white blanket and spread it on the floor and began to help calm me. Meanwhile, Phil kept insisting that I lie down on the birthing bed so that he could examine me vaginally. As with Nat's birth, the one position I couldn't tolerate was flat on my back. At that point the contractions were only three minutes apart, and I resumed the kneeling position for each one. Phil finally gave up.

Soon Evelyn Myskow, a registered nurse who had been trained as a midwife in Scotland, came on the scene, and my wish to have my baby delivered by a midwife was fulfilled. It was even done legally!

Whenever the pain threatened to overwhelm me I would stare out the window at the sun-stained peaks and breathe in their strength. Pat stayed with me through it all, breathing with me and reassuring me the way that Jay had done during Nat's birth. Her back massage was indispensable, and I didn't realize until later, when she broke into tears, how intense the experience had been for her.

The nurses urged me to lean back, but after two grueling hours of steady pushing, I stubbornly pulled myself into a squatting position, and Ben was born. It was 4 p.m. Throughout labor Evelyn had done a great deal of vaginal massage, and even though Ben was a hefty nine pounds, eight and a half ounces, I didn't tear at all. It made me realize that with patience, episiotomies might not always be necessary. Since I was the only "patient" in the hospital and it was completely natural, it was the next best thing to a home birth. I was relieved to have had Ben in town. Because he was such a large baby, I might have panicked at home. Also I learned that he had a hernia that would have to be surgically repaired in Smithers in six months. My one regret was that Jay hadn't been present.

When I talked to Natalia an hour later on the telephone and told her that she had a baby brother she issued a dramatic sigh and said, "Oh no!"

With remarkable foresight, blonde-haired blue-eyed Ben saved his first smile for Natalia when she came with Pat to see him, and he was begrudgingly granted a place in her heart.

A week later the Grues were kind enough to loan their truck to a friend named Ron, who drove us home. Ron took his malamute dog and sled along and maneuvered the awkward load down the trail. Ben rode in a pack strapped to my front and Nat walked ahead. Tall spruce pierced the hauntingly blue sky and squirrels scampered over the freshly fallen snow. Nat was so happy to get home that she ran the last length of the snowy trail.

A large fir bough wreath with a red bow adorned the log wall below the kitchen window. At first my spirits fell because I didn't see any smoke coming out of the chimney. Then at the sound of Nat's shouts Jay came bursting out of the cabin. A smile lit up his face, which was bushy and gaunt after six weeks of solitude.

Only a couple of days earlier, Jay had met a worker from the highways department on the road who had told him that we had a son. Up until then Jay had known nothing. When I carefully lifted the blanket so that Jay could see our baby, Ben's pupils slowly slid toward his nose, making him resemble a goofy little gnome. I assured Jay, somewhat defensively, that they would straighten out.

Despite the glow from our homecoming, the inside of the cabin looked dingy to me after living in Pat's gleaming house. The main floor of the addition was still dirt, and because the running water system that Jay had installed was frozen, the earth floor was cluttered with buckets. While other women dreamed of microwave ovens beneath the Christmas tree, I dreamed of boards beneath my chair. Jay had also taken in a roommate recently. A sick chicken sat in a cage in the corner. Also during our absence Jay had made me a fine writing desk, using our little table top for the surface. We placed it upstairs beside the south-facing window. Downstairs was a new dining table and also a table and chair set for Nat's dolls. How could I complain? Life was mainly good. With the arrival of our son, our family was complete, and for now our home in the woods was safe from the flames of government persecution.

Chapter 5

Feeding the Family

L IKE NATALIA, BEN thrived on mainly breast milk until age two. His eyes straightened out a couple of weeks after he was born and turned a dark striking brown, while his hair transformed to sunny blond. He was a cheerful fellow full of heart-melting smiles, though often a thorn in his sister's side. Her jealousy reared its green head regularly, and to make matters worse for Nat, Ben developed deep, endearing dimples that doubled his charm.

By the time Ben was two years old and a blockbusting thirty-five pounds, Nat was calling the shots. She would now and then feed him whole cloves of home-grown garlic, which he would obligingly munch on, his eyes watering only slightly.

Feeding our children was never a problem because we produced 75 percent of our food. Even though as self-appointed peasants our income was well below the poverty line, our children never knew hunger.

Most of our food was either grown in our gardens or gathered from the local forests. The items that we still needed to purchase were ordered from a grocery store in Terrace, 250 miles to the south. Transport trucks make regular runs up the Stewart-Cassiar Highway, and our supplies were trucked north and then dropped at the head of our trail. They were then backpacked down the three-mile path, or in winter Jay hauled them on the sled behind our Elan ski-doo. This trusty little work machine was purchased in 1982 after Jay's job with B.C. Hydro ended. Jay sometimes took the children on the sled behind the ski-doo, or else they hiked with me. Once the snow trail was well packed, it was smoother going than in the summer. But there were times that the ski-doo was taxed to its limits, and occasions when it simply couldn't navigate the trail at all. Often I used a kik-sled, a Norwegian-made sled with metal runners that operates much like a scooter and moves swiftly once a kick, glide, kick, glide rhythm is established. The wooden framework extends into handles, and there is a seat for a child. On the way home into the valley—a gradual descent—we sped home in forty minutes.

At the trailhead was a cut into the trees, the result of an error when the highway was being built. This level landing was where our visitors parked and also where we stored supplies in a makeshift shelter before packing them down the trail.

From the trailhead it was sixty-five miles north to a native village called Iskut, and 120 miles north to Dease Lake. Ninety miles south was Meziadin Junction—little more than a truck stop and highways camp. From there the highway branched off and traveled thirty miles west to Stewart, where we had a post office box. Every three months or so I hitchhiked in for mail and to visit my friends. Jay sometimes went more frequently, so we usually didn't have to wait more than six weeks to receive mail. Since letters were my only link with a whole network of friends and correspondents, they were a vital part of my life. The workers in Stewart's tiny post office frequently breathed a sigh of relief when they saw us coming, so anxious were they to clear their shelves of accumulated letters and magazines. We also received library books by mail—another weighty bundle to pack home. Since most of our supplies were ordered from Terrace, on trips to Stewart I picked up luxury items such as cheese and fresh fruit. All supplies, of course, had to be packed down the trail. Being small, the most I could carry at one time was a forty-five-pound bag of chicken feed, and I did this at times.

I spent at least four hours a day preparing meals, baking, and, in season, canning. Natalia and Ben were usually close by, and I enjoyed the family warmth as well as the heat from the cookstove.

On a shopping trip to Smithers in 1980, Jay and I had picked out what we considered to be the Rolls Royce of wood cookstoves. The Findlay oval from Elmira, Ontario—a large, cast-iron, chrome-plated model—came complete with hot-water reservoir and warming oven. We had it transported up the highway by freight truck, then hired a helicopter working in the area to fly it the last three miles. Once installed, it quickly became the heart of our home. In the morning the house didn't come to life until the stove was contentedly crackling and growling as it consumed the birch, balsam, spruce, and pine that we fed it. Once the air was lacked with the smell of coffee and I was dishing up steaming bowls of porridge and raisins—which we bought from the Terrace Co-op—Natalia and Ben would come wearily down the stairs, Ben often with a dream to tell, and Nat usually looking for Pippin, the cat. Pippin was willing to risk being stepped on for the luxury of curling up to the black stove-beast, whose kettle purred maternally. Nat would scoop her up, but even as she cuddled her, in the back of her mind was Cindy, the fluffy gray cat she had had for six years and who was nabbed by wolves just before she was about to give birth to her first litter.

Our diet was dictated by the seasons, and despite the absence of oranges from Florida and lettuce from California, we stayed healthy. After a long root crop–dominated winter, we eagerly reached for spring's first green onions. As a toddler, Ben ate onions with as much gusto as he gobbled garlic. In addition to the crops we raised largely for storage, throughout the growing season we also feasted on numerous varieties of lettuce as well as spinach, Brussels sprouts and other brassicas, and mounds of asparagus. We didn't stop enjoying the festival of delights picked fresh from the garden until snow concealed the last leaves of kale.

Then we trudged to the root cellar for prime potatoes, carrots, beets, turnips, parsnips, celery, and cabbage and to the cupboards for jars of moose, bear, and trout as well as peas, beans, pickles, berries, rhubarb, jams, and jellies. Dried parsley, onions, celery, sage, dill, wild Canada mint, oregano, thyme, peas, beans, and zucchini contributed to our winter meals. We went through our lean times too, when we ran out of meat, but those spells deepened our appreciation for times of plenty.

The top of the cookstove was never more crammed with pots than in canning season. The centerpiece was the substantial pressure cooker. The log walls of our home became permeated with the aroma of the red bubbling brew as I stirred raspberry jam in a large kettle.

From the surrounding woods we gathered wild raspberries, highbush cranberries, lowbush cranberries, gooseberries, rose hips, and currants. The wild berry that we treasured most was the Black Mountain huckleberry. About twenty miles to the north, in the Iskut burn that sprawled like a huge gray beast clutching the mountainsides, huckleberries abounded. We all looked forward to our excursions there each August and September. Beneath the wind-whittled carcasses of standing dead trees, with enchanting ridges winding off into the distance, we gathered hundreds of pounds of berries, many as big as grapes. Natalia and Ben were always eager to fill their "stomach buckets" first, their pleasure displayed in deep purple smiles. After toting our bounty home, we canned some of it in a light sugar syrup for winter fruit and made some into a rich jam. A portion was dried for a concentrated trail snack or a zesty addition to cakes or muffins. The remainder was eaten fresh or baked into pies.

The rest of the produce for canning we grew. From the end of April until late October, our lives revolved around the garden, a patchwork of plots fit snugly against the meandering Natty Creek. We relied heavily upon it as the source of all our vegetables, herbs, and flowers, and much of our berries and grain.

When Jay had first arrived, no gardens existed within a hundred miles and he had had to experiment to find suitable varieties of crops that would adapt to a land of extremes, where frost can occur at any time of the year. Jay had been keeping weather records for the Atmospheric Environmental Service since 1977, and we had never known it to go higher than 90°F or lower than minus 37°. Being near 57° north latitude, even though we were tucked in at an elevation of fourteen hundred feet above sea level and surrounded by six-thousand- to seven-thousand-foot mountains, we had sunlight in the garden for about sixteen hours a day during May, June, and July.

All the soil was turned by hand until 1982, when the purchase of a rotary tiller brought much of this back-wrenching work to an end. Gradually we expanded Jay's original fifty- by a hundred-foot plot to close to three acres. The black alluvial soil of the Ningunsaw Valley was rich with nutrients, and we organically grew all our crops, including three thousand to four thousand pounds of potatoes. By the time Ben was three years old he was able to gobble three whole potatoes at a sitting, and they remain a favorite food for both children. We found the stone-free riverbottom soil to be ideal for all root crops. We were lucky enough to start out with near ideal soil conditions and it was our aim to maintain that fertility through the use of compost and mulch.

Frost posed no threat to brassicas, and we were able to grow cauliflower the size of dinner plates and giant cabbages. We were also lucky enough to harvest tender broccoli from July until late October. In addition, by starting seeds indoors and covering the plants once they were set out in the garden, we raised small quantities of sweet corn, tomatoes, bush beans, and cucumbers. Annually we produced about three hundred pounds of wheat, twenty-five pounds of poppy seed, and limited amounts of oats, barley, and experimental grains. The wheat we either parched and ground for cereal or ground into flour for bread. The children witnessed the whole process of making bread—beginning with wheat sown in the field and ending with plump loaves emerging from the pans. Nat learned to make bread when she was eight years old, and hers now rivals mine for quality and flavor.

Each spring our eyes were dazzled and our souls nourished by the sight of thousands of crocuses, daffodils, tulips, grape hyacinths, pansies, calendulas, irises, and lilies that unfurled their brilliance below in the garden.

Jay remained chief gardener, but in order to cope with the demands of such a large garden the whole family had to pitch in. Some of the work they considered fun, like dancing all over the freshly planted wheat fields to pack them down. And Ben would squat his way down a three-hundred-foot furrow, methodically pressing pea-sized garlic bulbils into the soil while I did the same across from him. He liked to chat while we planted, and I ignored his irregular spacing and slowed my pace slightly in consideration of his smaller, less experienced hands.

Fall harvest season was the most hectic time, and it could consume every waking moment. In 1986, when Natalia was six years old, she was unexpectedly relieved of her part in it. My sister Donna, her husband Rick, and sons Isaac, Dorian, and Tennessee came to visit, and on August 19 Natalia traveled south back to the Shuswap area with them. Nat would return with my mother, who paid us an annual visit in September. After waving good-bye to Nat and the others, I cried as I trudged back down the trail with Ben and our black Lab pup, Lulu. I knew that I would miss Natalia terribly. I often needed to express my thoughts, but as the years went by I was becoming increasingly reluctant to try to talk to Jay. So often my words were met with denunciation or, at best, cool patronage. Despite her age, Natalia had become my main companion. It was a very lonely life in many ways. But I wanted Nat to have this experience and I trusted my family completely with her. And this would mean quality time for Ben. Our son wasn't yet walking but would accompany us on all our berry-picking excursions. During Nat's absence we hiked to Bob Quinn Lake twice to harvest lowbush cranberries. Ben loved the canoe, and his favorite position while we were moored was to fold himself perfectly in half over the edge of it with both plump feet off the bottom, his fat hands stretched out flat feeling the motion of the water, and his head so close to the lake that now and then he trailed his hair through it. First picking a spot clean, I'd plunk Ben on a hassock of moss in the sunshine and gather the surrounding cranberries. Moving him along, I would gradually work my way around the island. The lake caught and held autumn's first splashes of gold from the overhanging birch trees, and a loon couple came close and released their cries while a hawk spiraled up the clear indigo sky.

The weeks sped by, and the root cellar was stuffed and our shelves were lined with a colorful array of preserves by the time Nat and Ben's Grandma Lorna and her friend, Armour, brought Nat home in early September. Natalia was overjoyed to be home, and she was unusually attentive toward her little brother—especially if it was time to focus on correspondence lessons.

As autumn deepened the rain descended. To our horror, logging had begun not far from our home, and Natty Creek had become erratic and muddy whenever it rained. The café au lait–colored stream was swollen beyond its banks in places, and the roar of the Ningunsaw River could easily be heard inside the house. The birch, poplar, and cottonwood were like golden lamps lit in the medley of spruce and mist.

As I stirred huge pots of raspberry and huckleberry jam and chopped zucchini for pickles, Jay fit the last rocks into the retaining wall. Nat drew owls and wolves with "Save the Wildlife" printed above their heads, and baby Ben indulged in stepping sprees, tottering around a little more each day with a comical Frankenstein gait.

Each year, one of the greatest gardening challenges facing us was the reversal of seasonal rains. Rather than being blessed with spring rains, we endured spring droughts and fall downpours. We coped with this by harvesting as much as we could at the first sign of a dry day in late summer and early autumn.

Never were the kids and I more involved with the harvest than in 1991, when Natalia was eleven and Ben was five. Jay, who usually did most of the heavy work, had taken a surveying job on the Iskut Road, which was being built two miles downstream from us. The thought of a road slicing into one of the few remaining wilderness areas in British Columbia infuriated me, and I was distressed by Jay's decision to work for the "intruders." At the same time, I knew that, as a staunch defender of the patriarchy, he would not be swayed by my opinion.

All summer 1991, while Jay was surveying on the Iskut Road, the sky hung like soggy cotton above the black spruce spires, releasing frequent showers, which collected in puddles in the garden. Jay harvested as much as he could when he returned home in the evenings and on his days off. In this way we managed to bring in all the grain and some of the other crops, but the substantial remaining portion of a huge harvest hung around my neck like a lead weight. Just shelling the peas for a full batch of canning took Nat, Ben, and me four hours, and picking, shelling, and processing them consumed the better part of a day. Still, Nat and Ben stuck by me, and the only task they balked at was raspberry picking, since they weren't keen on scrambling through the brush and bugs. The previous spring, Jay had ordered honeybees—nature's great pollinators—from a beekeeper in Stewart. This year the raspberries were more prolific than ever, and I found it impossible to keep up with them on my own. But Nat and Ben were right with me as I dug potatoes, our hands forming shovels and burrowing into the soil in search of riches—Red Norland, Kennebec, Yukon Gold, and more.

"Yuck!" the kids complained when their fingers pierced a slimy mother potato whose strength and essence had been transmitted to her offspring. As we labored, the knees of our jeans grew black, and stiffness crept into shoulders and buttocks. Ben went soberly about his task, and I scarcely saw his eyes at all due to his strong attachment to a low-riding orange tie-dyed baseball cap brought by my mother on one of her visits. Ben was so in love with it that he even wore it to bed at night.

No matter how large the work load, the children always found time to play. Nat and Ben discovered that the soft garden soil was the ideal place to practice handstands, and when they weren't bending to pull beets or bunches of clover for rabbit food, they were flinging their hands at the earth and their feet into the air. Every time I glanced up I would see either Nat or Ben gleefully upside down, their bare feet planted in the sky and trying their utmost to stay there. I hated to bring them back to earth with more chores, but I simply couldn't do it all on my own.

Natty and I struggled up the drizzly slope to the root cellar with a bulging five-gallon bucket of carrots in each earth-stained hand, our arms threatening to release from their sockets. With the knowledge that there were still a thousand pounds to go, my long-legged daughter showed the strain. But as I watched Nat hoist full buckets over the sides of waist-high cellar bins, I realized that at eleven she was every bit as strong as I was.

Our root cellar was nothing more than an underground log cabin with a two-inch air vent leading to the surface, but it kept our vegetables in prime condition from one growing season to the next. Excess produce was used to feed our domestic chickens, geese, and rabbits, which provided fresh eggs and meat, skins and down, and manure for fertilizer.

In this life-style, it was inevitable that our children had witnessed the birth and death of animals, both wild and tame. It was not easy for Natalia, who has always felt a deep affinity with animals, particularly chickens. It is wise advice never to name your food, yet Nat named and loved every chicken (with the exception of one) that ever lived in the Ningunsaw Valley, and she was an expert on their individual personalities. They trusted her enough to lay warm wet eggs into her waiting hand.

From the time she was three, we were accustomed to seeing Nat walking about packing full-sized roosters, alert but submissive, in her small arms. Personally, I never felt relaxed around any rooster, but one in particular, a bird called Avalanche, was too nasty to gain even Nat's affection.

It was a bright spring in 1984, and we were in possession of an old 1969 Chrysler (which I had bought from my brother on a visit to Shuswap Lake) and an extra ten dollars. We were on our way home from Stewart when Jay, Nat (then four years old), and I called on some gentlefolk who were living in a teepee. The yard was a clutter of ducks, chickens, and geese, and Natalia felt at home right away. Before we left we purchased a rooster who was being persecuted by his brothers.

We crated up the martyr, placed him on the broad backseat, and Natalia cheerfully climbed in and sat beside him. Smugly, we rattled our way north toward our bush home. Livestock was nearly impossible to obtain in this remote region, and for many months we had been wanting a rooster.

Upon first perusal, the rooster looked like a prime specimen. Jay, who was also a poultry fancier as a child, assured me that this bird would be good breeding stock. The extra large Cornish-Rock was snowy white with scarlet eyes and comb, which had wilted slightly under the trauma of transport. On the trip home over the rough gravel road, I turned frequently and smiled obsequiously at him, more to put myself at ease than for his benefit. I had had a typical small Canadian town upbringing in which roosters were merely the clay ornaments on the top kitchen shelf or the proud feathered birds that crowed at dawn from the creaking pages of children's books. I wasn't at all comfortable with the real thing. Little did I know how much, with the passage of time, our rooster's evil proportions would expand in all our imaginations.

With prescience, we called the new bird Avalanche. He instantly adjusted to his new surroundings, and after putting the flock of ten hens in line he took to strutting and flapping about the chicken yard. The violent beating of his wings resounded menacingly. He mated with the hens methodically, always catching them off guard. He'd hit them full force from behind, and they'd slide into the dust of the coop. (Natalia was disgusted with him and would try, without success, to intervene.) With only a hint of indignation, the hens would rise, shake, and compose themselves. With each fresh assault Avalanche sounded his victory crow from what came to be his favorite pedestal, the top of the compost heap. His crow invariably started off in fine form until he hit the last two notes, at which point his voice would fade out altogether. Any less obstinate neck would have ruptured from the strain that he placed on it in his attempt to pump out the missing notes. However, this never prevented him from delivering his demented bugle call.

His treatment of the hens led to the demise of the most splendid bird of the flock—Natty's favorite, which she had affectionately dubbed Daffy. Daffy's red feathers gleamed golden in the sun, her comb was bright and as uniform as rickrack, and she was plump and voluptuous. Avalanche singled her out immediately. He'd descend upon her in a torrent of libido, ripping feathers out of her neck in his enthusiasm. The other hens, jealous of Daffy because she received most of Nat's attention, welcomed an excuse to pick on her. After Avalanche had cleared a patch at the back of her neck, the other hens began to attack the bald spot, and it was downhill from there for Daffy. She instantly fell to the bottom of the pecking order and was soon the eyesore of the flock, with naked patches and broken feathers. Only Natalia remained devoted to her.

My first violent confrontation with Avalanche occurred one afternoon when I went into the coop to collect the eggs. The flock was busy scratching in the dirt, but when I reached into the first nest, suddenly I heard a stampede of feet coming from behind and *whomp!* I screamed as a beak and two feet simultaneously struck my derriere. Avalanche attacked with the force and skill of a karate expert. The three-point strike resulted in a triangle of bruises and an increased reluctance on my part to venture toward the laying nests.

Being petite, I am used to standing beside humans who remind me of my stature, but a rooster who made me feel small was too much to bear. I tried arming myself with a shovel before entering the coop, but he'd fly over and attack anyway, his beak and feet ringing against it, like a victory gong. He must have sensed that I was afraid of him, and his crimson eyes grew redder and crazier, drunk with power.

As a parent, I'm fully aware that it is bad policy to require your children to do what you yourself are afraid to do, but I found myself asking Nat, in a sugary voice, if she would like to collect the eggs.

Avalanche was bigger than Nat, and I loathed myself as I watched from the safe side of the fence while my four-year-old daughter scurried over to the nest. Her waist-length hair was braided and she wore a sundress. When Avalanche charged, as he routinely did when a back was turned, Nat whirled around, held her arms straight out, and rushed toward him shouting like a bantam warrior. I watched with amazement as the tyrant turned tail and ran. Natalia calmly went about her business gathering the eggs.

However, the next day when I tried the same tactic, Avalanche didn't retreat. Once again he struck with beak and spur-studded feet. When I complained to Jay about the unruly rooster, he replied, "Well, he isn't going to kill you!" I had my doubts.

Avalanche waited for his chance to get revenge on Natty. As she stood in the coop with her back turned one morning, the thundering of small fierce feet unexpectedly culminated in a blow to her back that landed her flat on her face in the dirt. Nat didn't cry, but the words that stormed out of her mouth should not have been in the vocabulary of a four-year-old.

One day the foreman from the highways camp, his wife, and their five-year-old son and three-year-old daughter arrived for a visit. It was their first trip to our wilderness home. As they stood near the fence and gazed rapturously at the green blush of young wheat and barley in the garden below and the monarch spruce and towering snow-wreathed mountains beyond, a low rumble sounded from behind. Without warning, Avalanche charged the crowd, his feet and beak landing squarely on the back of their small unsuspecting daughter, knocking her flat. Less stoic than Nat, she wailed loudly. Nat tore after Avalanche, but the damage had already been done.

Early one morning in July, when the yard was full of the smell of wild roses and bird song, I quietly opened the door and peeked left, then right. Avalanche was nowhere in sight. I pulled the neck of my full-length housecoat closed against the crisp air. The clear sky held bright promise of a beautiful day. In one hand I carried a bucket of "night waters," which we routinely poured over the compost heap to aid in the decomposition of organic matter. Suddenly out of nowhere appeared Avalanche, first strutting and then charging toward me at top speed, his scarlet eyes possessed. Alarmed, and with the folds of my housecoat flapping around me, I flew to the top of a nearby stump. There I stood helplessly clutching my bucket while Avalanche, comb flopping over one eye like a beret and spurs gleaming in the sun, patrolled near the base. I wondered how long I was going to be stranded on the stump and considered shouting for help. Then I remembered that I had but one weapon available. I leered down at the rogue that had bullied me mercilessly all these weeks and thought, why not? With a single motion I dumped the entire contents of the pail over his feathered finery and instantly doused his cockiness. Avalanche eventually resumed his tyranny, and none of us felt remorseful when, after several seasons, the vicious bird was beheaded and made into stew.

Ben shared my trepidation when it came to feathered tormentors. In April 1991 I was cleaning up the yard when I became aware of a strange noise. It took me a few moments to realize that it was Ben, age five, crying in absolute terror. Dashing over, I found him backed against the freshly stacked woodpile lining the outside kitchen wall, held captive by Gandhi, our ornery gander. The plump white bird, every bit as tall as Ben and twice as terrible in Ben's eyes as Avalanche had been in mine, was viciously biting him. Meanwhile the geese hens, Stupid, Dub Dub, and Loud Mouth, stood on the sidelines like cheerleaders, honking him on. Ben's big dark eyes were filled with fear, and other than wailing at the top of his lungs, he made no attempt to defend himself. Normally I made a wide detour around ganders too. Their bills could deliver a pinch as powerful as a pair of strong pliers, and their wings packed a wallop that could break an arm. However, when I saw my son being attacked, I shoved my way through the fat and feathers of the hens, seized their leader by his snakelike neck, and hoisted him up while his flat pink feet paddled helplessly in the air. He was lighter than I expected. One cold, yellow-rimmed, blue eye regarded me for a split second before I sent him sailing far out into the yard. The hens quickly waddled away from the woodpile, gabbing about this turn of events.

At that time I couldn't have imagined crying over anything that happened to Gandhi, but a year later my sentiments changed. One May night, an hour and a half after we had gone to bed, I was yanked out of a deep sleep by pandemonium from the goose residence under the eaves outside the east corner of the house. The nest containing newly hatched goslings was in the farthest corner of the L formed by the old and new wings of our dwelling, where the roof line descended to within two feet of the ground and provided a safe nook. Or so we thought. Geese can be hysterical at the best of times, but there was an authentic tone of desperation and also an oddly receding *honk honk honk*. The clamor woke Jay up as well, and he leapt downstairs in his shorts and T-shirt. His feet were bare. Dashing out onto the front porch, Jay could see by starlight the white form of a goose, on the far side of the creek, traveling swiftly across the garden. With a jolt he realized that Gandhi was not running through the night but was locked in the jaws of a fleeing wolf, whose form merged with the darkness. As Jay began to shout and holler, Natalia snapped awake. Ben slept on.

Jay flew upstairs and threw on clothes and boots. Rushing downstairs to the porch, I held a spotlight for him while he dashed through the garden, frantic to find Gandhi or at least some indication of his fate. Before he had even reached the greenhouse, I spotted our lordly gander standing in the middle of the creek in front of the twin giant spruce. From my vantage point there was no indication at all that he was hurt, but close up, Jay found him in sad shape. His beak was broken and torn at the end, and gurgling sounds emerged with each breath. Jay urged him upstream past the blood-smeared log bridge, and then as gently as he could he packed him up the hill and put him with his mate and babies. Grabbing the rifle, Jay hopped onto the front porch. It was a cool, damp night, and Nat and I shivered as we stood there barefoot. With the aid of the spotlight we could see two sets of eyes glowing from 250 yards away in the shrubby growth in front of the forest that surrounded our clearing. We discovered that one pair belonged to our tomcat, Winkin. Swinging the spotlight to the left, we illuminated a large black wolf. Jay raised the rifle and fired. He missed, and as he reloaded the gun the culprit snuck away.

At that time we had goslings, cats and kittens, baby bunnies, and also chicks hatching out. We were all uneasy as Nat and I crawled back into bed. Jay announced that he was going to stay up all night. As he declared, Gandhi was his friend. Four years earlier he had ordered the Embden gander through the Terrace Co-op from a hatchery in Vernon, British Columbia. Gandhi's first flight in life was by jet as a day-old gosling. He flew from Vernon to Terrace, and then the co-op sent him 250 miles north by freight truck. He rode the last three miles with nine other goslings in a box on Jay's back.

When Gandhi was ten months old he began his courtship with Dub Dub, and each year they became more successful at raising goslings. It was with real pleasure that we viewed the proud gander and hen with their band of little yellow-gray fluff-ball goslings.

Naturally Gandhi was most aggressive during breeding season, and then it was unwise to come within twenty feet of him. He could rock across the yard at an incredibly fast rate, gaining speed all the way, his neck snaking out menacingly, his bill agape and issuing a steaming *hisssss*. If he managed to get a good hold with his beak, he would flail at his victim simultaneously with his wings, striking with the hard leading edge. However, once the hens were settled on their eggs, Gandhi would become lonely. This coincided with planting time, and more than once Gandhi waddled down the hill after us on bright orange feet and followed us into the garden. He would amble close and regard us with a bright blue eye. The kids and I gazed back skeptically, suspicious of this change in his personality. Once Nat was crouching down transplanting chives when Jay fired up the rotary tiller. In an effort to get away, Gandhi climbed right onto her back.

Being the only gander available, one season Gandhi bred with Dub Dub, Stupid, Pinhead, and Loud Mouth. However, no matter how lovely the other hens were, Gandhi's great love was Dub Dub. Even when the other single females were present he displayed completely biased adoration for her. The feeling was obviously reciprocated, and they were a close and devoted couple. Whenever they proudly patrolled the yard, Gandhi would position himself between us and his mate. At times his defensive behavior seemed ridiculous, as when he engaged in fierce battles with buckets and brooms, but the fact that he would protect his family against such impossible odds as a marauding wolf made him worthy of a great deal of respect.

The morning after the attack on Gandhi's life, I stepped outside to view our gander and was shocked by what I saw. His snowy feathers were smeared with blood, and he was standing beside Dub Dub and their blood-spattered two-day-old brood. Not so much as a hiss issued forth from his brutally split beak. What distressed me most were his eyes. Normally so bold, alert, and defiant, they were now sunken and dim. With tears streaming down my face I told him how sorry I was. When Dub Dub and her brood moved a short distance away, Gandhi, normally the fearless leader, meekly followed. I was moved by his stoic effort to fulfill his duty to stay with them, even though his strength failed him.

I longed for the return of Gandhi the Terrible. I also suffered a twinge of guilt, remembering the first time the wolf had showed itself. In January we had all watched the lone black creature stroll boldly across the frozen pond. Jay had wanted to shoot him, suspecting that he wasn't healthy. Natalia, Ben, and I, unconvinced that it was necessary, begged him to spare the animal. Then Spooky's (our scruffy black terrier's) moose bones began to disappear regularly. Next a whole moose hide, which Jay had been soaking to remove the hair, vanished from the tub near the pond. Another morning in March we discovered a well-packed wolf trail around the perimeter of the pond, while the geese loitered in the center where the ice had melted.

One day in April I was sitting in the guest cabin, located out of sight of the main house. It was a chilly morning. I was dressed all in wool from toque to heavy socks and was busy scribbling away on *Wilderness Mother*. Craving coffee, I was hoping that Natalia would soon arrive promised thermos. A movement outside the window snagged ation, and I caught a flash of black, which I thought was Spooky. Glancing up I was startled to see that my visitor was the black wolf. It was only about four feet away. As it strolled slowly past I had plenty of time to observe it. Its somewhat scruffy-looking coat was flecked with lighter-colored hair, and its yellow eyes contained a cool wildness. When I tapped on the window, it quickened its pace but didn't flee.

Creeping over to the door, I peered through the small central window and was jolted to see the wolf standing in front of the two steps leading up to the cabin's door. It didn't appear nervous. It merely stood there scanning its surroundings with untamed golden eyes. I kept a tight grasp on the door handle while I watched it linger there for several minutes. Then, spotting my face in the glass, it trotted west toward a favorite moose haunt called Willow Park, and its dark form was soon swallowed by the trees.

But when I opened the door and descended the steps a few moments later, I saw the wolf standing on the other side of the cabin only twenty feet away. Evidently it had circled and snuck back through the timber. As it stared at me with an uncanny familiarity, I suddenly remembered that Natalia was due to arrive at any moment. A split second later I spotted her and Spooky advancing through the trees. "Natalia!" I screamed out in warning.

"You better get out of here!" I hollered at the wolf. All too casually it trotted as far as the base of the hillside, only abut forty feet away, and stood staring back at me. While the "big bad wolf" lurked close by I felt as helpless as granny as I waited for Little Red Riding Hood to arrive with my goodies. What worried me most was that this wolf appeared to have next to no fear of people.

Natalia continued toward the cabin and reached it safely while the wolf still lingered on the hillside. Nat reported that Spooky had started snorting and barking as soon as she got to the far garden, and a moment later Nat spotted the wolf watching her from behind a bush.

We had had no further sightings of the wolf until he attacked Gandhi. Despite the severe injuries Gandhi sustained, by the end of the next day our goose managed to release a hiss as Ben passed him. There seemed a slim chance that he might recover, but sadly, our hope did not live long.

The next day at 4 a.m. I heard a very weak *honk honk honk* fading off down the hill. I tore out of bed and downstairs. Fumbling my way through the door, I stepped out into inky blackness. I knew that Dub Dub had bedded down with her brood right on the back doorstep, and naturally Gandhi would be nearby. We were certain that no wild animal would venture that close. To my astonishment I couldn't find any adult geese. Normally even in the darkness the snowy white birds bloomed with brightness.

Stumbling over to the nest site, I discovered seven goslings huddled together in terror. I rushed onto the front porch and shone the spotlight down on the garden. To the west I caught a flash of eyes. Swinging the light to a location directly below our attached greenhouse, I spotted a flurry of feathers beside the creek.

By then Jay, armed with a rifle, and Natalia were up. With the spotlight we once again picked out a pair of glowing eyes on the far side of the creek and outermost edge of the clearing. Jay shot, but something must have deflected the bullet. The wolf fled. Nat and I held the light while Jay walked down and found, on the opposite side of the creek, a goose carcass that the wolf had been in the process of eating.

Taking a cardboard box outside, we carefully scooped up the seven three-day-old orphans and took them inside. Without their mother to keep them warm, they would soon die out in the elements.

Once they were settled, Natalia and I went back to bed while Jay, rifle in hand, and a reluctant Spooky followed a trail of goose feathers. Dawn was breaking by then, and the feathers led them through the woods to the guest cabin and then across Natty Creek. Abruptly the feathers came to an end. If not for a keen sense of observation, Jay would never have discovered the burial site. The wolf had scraped the moss away, dug a grave, and deposited the goose in it. After covering his prize with earth, he had finished by carefully replacing the moss and packing it down over the top of it.

Jay soon pieced the story together. The wolf had come in and nabbed Dub Dub from the back step, killed her by the creek, and then carted her away to the cache that Jay had found. It wasn't until hours later that he had returned for Gandhi. I couldn't begin to imagine the despair that Gandhi must have endured as he helplessly watched his lady love being carried away. And it was Gandhi that the wolf was devouring on the far side of the creek. His death honks retreating into the damp darkness had awoken me.

Determined to catch the offender, Jay buried the carcasses in the garden with two wing feathers protruding and surrounded them with leg-hold traps. As much as I respected wild animals, I didn't feel safe with this one lurking in our midst. He was simply too bold, and the next victim could be Spooky or even Ben.

Three days later at 8 a.m. Jay hopped out of bed and strode to the window. "There's something in the trap," he announced. Springing over I looked down on the garden and saw a wide drag mark winding away from where the goose wings had been sticking out of the soil. There were only a few feathers left on the wings. The path ploughed by the poor beast hauling a fifty-pound snarl of traps crossed the tulip and daffodil rows, wiping out a few flowers, then wound through the mulch in the direction of the creek.

With hair askew and heavy eyes, Ben hopped from his bed and climbed on my desk to watch while Nat and I stood at the window. Jay had already dressed, grabbed the rifle, and gone. Unexpectedly we saw a chunk of garden soil near the creek start to move. An instant later we realized that it was the wolf! His hide blended perfectly with the earth.

As bad as I felt for the geese that he never got to eat, I felt equal pity for the wolf. When the wolf saw Jay with his gun he crept as fast as he could with his "ball and chain" to some raspberry bushes bordering the garden and cowered beneath them. From there he dragged himself to a spot in front of the new greenhouse (built near the giant twin spruce). As he lay almost flat, Jay shot him. Natalia turned away as Jay delivered a second and final bullet.

The wolf was a young male with past injuries, including a broken cheekbone, possibly from a moose kick, porcupine quills, and a recent bullet wound in his front foreleg. His teeth were in excellent condition, but the fact that he would return at all after being shot showed how hungry he was.

As for the goslings, thanks to a tiny bantam hen with a giant maternal instinct, they were well taken care of. Raina, a hawk-colored banty, had four of her own chicks, and at night when the whole comical brood ran to her for warmth and protection she'd patiently accommodate them. Natalia and Ben were amazed. They had never seen a hen spread herself so thin!

Jay skinned the wolf, and I said a little prayer as we buried him in the garden. I couldn't blame the beast for going after the geese. After all, he'd likely never seen such plump and delicious meals. It was sobering to realize that as long as one has domestic animals it is less possible to live in harmony with the wilds. Natalia and Ben shared my grief for the three creatures that had been laid to rest in our garden. How odd that geese and wolf, prey and predator, would now together be consumed by the soil, which would, in turn, feed us.

Chapter 6

Where the Wild Things Are

THE FOREST CREATURES who were our neighbors in the wilderness were of course never very far away. One day—I was eight months pregnant with Natalia at the time—we were strolling half-naked along the black sand of the river flat. Abruptly the dogs, Boomer, Penny, and Digadee, began to bark in the direction of the cottonwood and spruce trees on the north bank. Suddenly a loud roar resounded and an enormous moose came charging toward us. I felt extremely vulnerable as over a thousand pounds of outraged animal tore after Boomer, who was heading straight back to us. As the moose advanced, our unborn child frantically kicked me from the inside, as though urging me to get the devil out of there! In defense Jay shouted and waved his arms widely. Only a few yards away from us, the moose veered to the left and plunged into a channel of the Ningunsaw River. There she stood thigh deep in water while the three dogs yapped savagely at her. As Jay settled on a cottonwood log to watch her, I cradled my belly in my arms to comfort the child who hadn't yet emerged into the light of day and yet was so profoundly there.

The hair along the moose's spine was standing straight up and she kept peering intently toward the timber, where we realized her calf quietly waited. We were now out of her limited range of vision and she had lost interest in us. Finally the dogs retreated and she made her way back to the place in the trees from which she had first appeared.

Growing up the realm of wild creatures, sightings and encounters were a part of our children's lives. Still, even when living in the middle of the bush, wild animals aren't spotted every day, and in this age of dwindling species, each visit was seen by the children for what it was— a gift and a privilege. Except, of course, when the occasional creature, driven by hunger, attempted to make a meal of our small livestock.

For Natalia, one of the most memorable encounters transpired when she was four years old. That March, the yard in front of our cabin was unexpectedly filled with a giant flock of crossbills and pine siskins. The small seed-eating birds descended in the hundreds. There were males in scarlet that deepened with age and countless olive-gray females. Also found among their ranks were the more flamboyant white-winged crossbills, with ebony and white wings against red. The air rang with their song, and every time we opened the front door vast numbers would explode into the air. The front yard was a solid shifting carpet of them.

With a wool coat tugged over her gingham dress and her hair in braids, Natalia sprinkled salt out in front of the house for the birds. Flocks of sixty crossbills swooped down to feed while masses more possessed the nearby trees. Aptly named, the birds have crossed bills, an adaptation for eating seeds. They rubbed their beaks along the boards placed in front of the house, their bright tongues flickering out to lap up the salt.

Natty and I would sit statue-still on the front step and wait for the crowds of crossbills to alight. In a matter of minutes we were surrounded, and as though mistaking our legs and feet for curious roots, they set down on them. Nat suppressed a giggle as one tried to perch on my head. I felt its little claws and the flutter of wings through my hair. Natalia would hide beneath an old gray blanket, spying through a peephole while crossbills and pine siskins landed on what must have appeared to them to be a somewhat bizarre rock.

The vast congregation of crossbills and siskins continued their vibrant song, swooping about the yard in vivid clouds. Frequently they took solo flights, like falling leaves, alone to their destination, but they were ever watchful, ready to respond to the dictations of the group. When one sensed danger they all flew up simultaneously.

With such large numbers there were inevitably a few accidents, and Natalia and I felt terrible when a bird crashed into our front window. With eyes clenched closed, the little seed eaters looked as though they had terrible headaches. Cradling the victims in our hands, Nat and I would stroke their bright feathers in sympathy. We could feel the tiny hearts beating inside the small warm bodies. We could offer little besides a soft touch and tone. Sometimes we had three or four sitting on the windowsill at once, the window ajar so that they could escape. Nat and I stroked them gently and talked to them, and one by one they recovered, the wilds leaping back into their eyes. With whirring wings they flew to the ragged birch trees on the edge of the hill.

One afternoon when Nat and I returned from the outhouse, a pine siskin was lying breast up, with its eyes closed, upon the rocks. I thought at first that it was dead, but when I picked it up it stirred. I laid it in a leather glove on the workbench and Nat kept a vigil while I went back to making bread. Before long it was sitting up, but when it tried to fly away it fell instead to the rock floor below. It had a broken wing. Nat cried as it floundered, afraid that it would hurt itself even more. Carefully she set out dishes of salt and water for it. It sat there a long while before hobbling off to find salt in the yard. Every few steps it would attempt to use both wings and would roll over in the process. Healthy siskins lit near it and then flew away again, abandoning it to its fate. Nat, in red tights, wool plaid dress, and gum boots, followed along beside it fretting. Soon it disappeared under the log fence and may have floundered down the hill and into the creek.

Natalia had witnessed death in animals before, but she had difficulty accepting that there was nothing we could do to help the pine siskin, especially after it vanished from sight. A few days later when a crossbill died, she carefully placed it in a box, dug a little hole in the yard near the rain gauge, and buried it. On top of the grave she placed an arrangement of wildflowers.

The giant flocks lingered in our clearing for about six months. Compared to the crossbills, the siskins were unspectacular in their gray, white, and yellow streaks. As the seasons advanced, the crossbills gradually flew away, like bright flowers, leaving behind the siskin foliage.

Over the years we enjoyed visits from numerous birds, including robins, warblers, sparrows, scores of songbirds, hummingbirds, great gray owls, whiskey jacks, ravens, ruffed grouse, swallows, red-winged blackbirds, bald eagles, hawks, and more. At times our pond lured down some exotic flying guests. One evening in October 1989 I was taking Ben to the outhouse when a strange *frank frank frank* sound yanked our attention upward. Against a pearly sky we saw the silhouette of a huge, long-necked bird with great slender legs trailing out behind it. We were eager to follow it over to the pond, and we scampered to the outhouse and back up the hill as quickly as we could. Excitement turned to disappointment when we scanned the calm pond and saw no sign of the bird. Back inside we discovered in a bird book that our visitor had been a great blue heron. Ben and Nat were amazed when I told them that these birds stand four feet tall and have a wingspan of six feet.

Later, we checked the pond again. In the gathering dusk, Ben's dark eyes shone as we spotted the heron standing quietly in one corner, remarkably spindly-legged and graceful. It appeared to be only ankle deep in the gleaming water. We froze, enchanted by the spectacle and honored to be so close to such a grand bird. Ben spoke and the startled heron took flight, soaring in a wide circle over the garden. Returning to the pond, it alighted on the central brush island. In the fading light, still as it was, it could easily have been mistaken for a crooked branch. The next morning at the first light of day its massive wings beat the air in farewell as it flew off to the south.

The pond also attracted merganser ducks, Canada geese, and once a trumpeter swan. Natalia, Ben, and I crept across the yard and sat quietly at the edge of the hill to observe our flighty guests. The snow-white trumpeter swan, with its jet-black beak that appeared riveted to its head by its equally black eyes, loitered about the pond for a full day and seemed unconcerned about our presence.

Nat and Ben didn't discriminate against smaller and less glamorous animal species. From age two on, Nat had a fascination for toads and Ben for bugs. I can still see Nat as a toddler, naked except for a red sunbonnet, crouching in the garden to catch a green or gold toad, its eyes bulging with fear. As she grew she learned the differences between frogs and toads and how to distinguish the males from the females. Nat also devised her own techniques for studying their habits. Turning them belly up in her hand, she would wait for a moment, and if the toad released a plaintive *peep-peep-peep*, she'd announce, "See? This one's a talker."

Ever since Ben was a toddler, if a bug crawled or flew into his field of vision, he was after it, plucking it gingerly with his small fingers, being careful not to crush it. He didn't flinch when a spider crawled up his arm or an earthworm wriggled about in his palm. Whenever he could manage it he would bring them back to show me, and we would study them together. I bought him a bug magnifier, a small clear plastic cylinder with a magnifying glass for a lid, and Ben would slip each hostage inside for a closer look and then finally let it go.

Even though its stay was brief, Natalia acquired a wild animal for a pet in 1985. In early July, when the wild roses bloomed in masses, Jay, Nat, and I were on our way down the drizzly river path when we saw a form huddled pathetically in the center of it, nearly concealed by the aromatic overhanging brush. When we got closer, we realized that it was a soaking wet woodchuck, not more than a month old. A large colony of them lived in the area, and even though they seldom bothered the garden, at times as many as eight would occupy front-row seats along a giant moss-cushioned log and watch us at work. This little fellow had obviously strayed from the fold and gotten himself lost. Natty issued a little moan of pity and approached him, but when she got too close he defended himself as best he could. Nat stopped cold when he lunged at her, "chucking" his sharp teeth and creating a rapid chattering sound.

We were all reluctant to approach him, but Nat pleaded with Jay to pick him up so that we could take him home and look after him. Jay obligingly removed his vest and grabbed the protesting creature gently but firmly with it. Nat decided that we'd call him "Chucky," and once he was in Jay's arms he was remarkably subdued. Chucky weighed only about one and a half pounds, and he had sharp gun-metal blue eyes, a ratlike face, small ears flattened back, and a bushy frosted coat. The fur on his belly was black with a reddish hue. Most fascinating of all were his paws, which were more like leathery little hands. His four "fingers" ended in long claws, while a pad on the palm side acted as a thumb.

After some deliberation we decided to carry him home and put him in with Porky and Bess, a pair of two-month-old rabbits living in a cage outside the woodshed. Unfortunately, Chucky wasn't impressed with rabbits at all and he hunkered down in a far corner, chattering his prominent teeth and lunging forward if they tried to get too close.

Natalia wanted very much to keep Chucky as a pet, but we knew that this wouldn't be possible if we couldn't get him to eat. He showed little interest in the greens we offered him. After supper we brought him indoors and all took turns holding him to get him accustomed to human handling. Jay and I were busy researching the diet of woodchucks in books as we sat at the table. Natalia, in long braids, was carefully holding Chucky. I had just finished reading aloud that they "eat only greens" when Nat took her bread crust from her plate. Chucky immediately grabbed it from her and started munching. Many milk-soaked chunks of bread later, we knew that woodchucks could acquire a taste for other foods.

Chucky always held on to his food with both paws while balancing on his haunches. Ever alert and aware of his surroundings, he relied more on his sight and hearing than on his sense of smell. Nat would scold him as he half climbed into his food bowl, greedily slurping up his food. At the best of times he was a remarkably noisy eater.

At Nat's insistence we decided that we would keep him, although we weren't sure what we would do with him between September and April when he wanted to hibernate. Suggestions ranged from the root cellar to a basket beside the fire. Certainly the food bill would never be high with him sleeping two-thirds of his life away. As it turned out, we never had to solve this problem. A week later my friend Pat's sister, Connie, her husband, Ken, and her eight-year-old daughter, Dawn Marie, came out from Stewart to visit. Dawn Marie was four years older than Nat and an animal lover too. The first attraction was Chucky, and they removed him from the cage to play with him. After carrying him around inside the house for a spell, they forgot about him. It was easy enough for Chucky to crawl beneath the floor of our then unfinished house and scurry on his way. With all the activity it was two hours before anyone even realized that he was gone. Later, after the company had left, Nat was very disappointed that she had lost her pet, but I tried to assure her that Chucky would be happiest to have his freedom and to find his way back to his own family.

The animals that most commonly wandered through our clearing or lingered to feed were moose and bears, but occasionally we saw wolves, weasels, porcupines, pine martens, mink, snowshoe hares, beavers, otters, and once a black fox.

The visitor that we trusted least was the black bear, and from May to October, each time we stepped outside we scanned the clearing and the hem of the woods for anything large and moving. After a long season on the alert, none of us were disappointed when the bears retired to their dens to dream the winter away. Still, sooner or later each spring one appeared in the garden. One year a bear made a mad dash through our goose pen, knocking down two sides and sending our birds to new heights of honking hysteria. At other times the geese remained strangely mute.

If I hadn't stepped out onto the porch one late summer evening in 1988 and looked down at the garden where the geese were penned, I would never have known that they were in trouble. In the violet light I saw a large, bulky black bear standing in the center of the pen devouring a goose from the head down. Meanwhile the rest of the gaggle was huddled in a corner, too terrified to let out a peep. I called my family and we all started to scream and holler and beat a triangle in an effort to scare the bear away. When nothing fazed it, Jay raced down the hill with a rifle and shot it. The only alternative would have been to stand helplessly by while it devoured, one by one, the remaining geese, which had been feasting all summer and were as plump as pincushions. When the bear fell, I rushed down the hill. Jay and I were distressed to see that our gander, Gandhi's predecessor, had been severely wounded. When he breathed, air hissed through an opening in his breast. Jay had no choice but to release him from his suffering. The bear made excellent burgers and roasts, and much of the meat was canned and fed us for many months.

Geese have a reputation of being good watchdogs, but they let us down another time as well. Ben was a baby and we were all snug in bed for the night. The huge rock retaining wall that Jay had built downstairs was complete except for a two-foot gap at the top that was closed in by a loose sheet of plastic. Just before we dropped off to sleep I heard a creepy scratching sound against the plastic. I nudged Jay, who assumed that it was Cindy, Natty's cat, trying to get in. He didn't want anything crawling over the surface of the wall since the mortar wasn't completely dry. Storming downstairs, he vowed to throw "that damned cat" out while Nat cringed in her bed praying for Cindy. A moment later Jay announced, "That's no cat. It's a bear!" In the shadows I could see Nat sitting bolt upright in her bed. While Jay stumbled for the gun I fumbled for the flashlight. Tripping downstairs, I held the flashlight while Jay loaded the gun. The bear had ripped a hole in the plastic over the west window. Jay told me to shine the light through the window while he poked the gun through the torn plastic and got ready to fire. A short distance away on the hillside I could see the bear's eyes glowing in the light. A blast from the gun sent him fleeing. By then Nat was on the stairs, and

Ben was awake too. We told her to stay inside with her brother while we went out and made sure that the animals were okay. As it turned out, the henhouse door was wide open, but they were all perched, still as stone, on their roost. It wasn't until several minutes later that we located the geese and our little black Lab, Lulu. Normally they didn't get along, but on this occasion they were all huddled in a corner under the eaves on the east side of the house. They were so silent that they seemed to be holding their breaths.

There are many different and conflicting theories about what to do if one encounters a bear. Some experts advise a person to yell loudly, while others say to talk softly to the bear. It has also been suggested that in the event of being chased it is best to drop your pack and head for the nearest tree. For many years this was dubious advice for me, since, more often than not, my pack contained a child. All schools of thought seem to converge on one point: Bears are unpredictable. Most often when walking through the woods the children were with me, and we talked and sang in order to let any bears in the neighborhood know that we were coming through. If bears have the option they will usually retreat. However, having a dog along can sometimes complicate the situation.

In May of 1989, Jay, Natalia, Ben, and I were on our way to Desiré Lake to go fishing. Ben was four years old then and capable of hiking on his own. The woods were slowly awakening to spring, and we hadn't yet seen any indication that the bears had emerged from hibernation. We had our scruffy but loyal little black terrier, Spooky, with us, and Ben and Nat were arguing about who was going to catch more fish. We had trudged up the first steep hill and were walking through the mossy woods, past the place where a large patch of lady's slipper blooms in June. Unexpectedly, Spooky burst into a frenzy of barking and dashed off into the woods to the right of the path, vanishing from sight. A minute later we heard a couple of loud cracks coming from the same direction. From out of the trees fled Spooky, her eyes full of terror and her legs a blur of speed. Directly behind and traveling just as quickly was a hefty black bear. Spooky's sole objective was to get back to us. My immediate concern was for Nat and Ben, small vulnerable figures between Jay and me. We were all momentarily overwhelmed by the sight of a full-sized bear charging straight toward us. Luckily, Jay broke through the paralysis of fear. He raised his arms well above his head in order to appear larger and began to shout loudly. Despite the racing of our hearts, we all joined in. Spooky collided with Jay's legs in her attempt to escape her pursuer. Within mere feet of us, the bear skidded to a jerky halt and then veered away into the woods. With stunned relief we stared at the prints left behind on the trail.

Luckily for the kids, such frightening encounters were balanced by more pleasant ones. In July 1991, Natalia, age eleven, Ben, age five, and I hiked up to Bob Quinn Lake to go swimming. With Nat at the bow and me at the stern, we paddled our canoe across the serene lake to tie up at the usual tattered birch tree that leaned far out over the water. The sky was pearly with huge black shifting clouds. Loons swam close by, their ethereal red eyes on us. Ben, in red cap and matching red T-shirt, had a perpetual smile on his face. After Nat and I swam and Ben had a swimming lesson, we headed back toward the bay where we had parked the canoe. On the way the wind rose and the water became so turbulent that paddling was difficult. Halfway back we pulled into a cove to rest.

Natalia immediately spotted a beaver lodge along the nearby eastern shore. Then on the opposite side of the canoe we were startled by a beaver swimming feverishly past us, its dark eyes glimmering in concentration. Since these creatures are nocturnal, we felt privileged to see one in the middle of the day. Unexpectedly, a peculiar noise called our attention back to the lodge. It sounded like many juvenile voices joined together in a musical chanting of *mmp-mmh mmp-mmh*. It resembled *ma-ma ma-ma*. Baby beavers! Ben appeared bewildered by it all but Nat's face shone with delight. Beavers bear their young between April and July, and normally they have two to four offspring, but sometimes up to eight. It sounded like at least six healthy voices issuing out of the center of the mound of mud and sticks. Suddenly the mama beaver gave a sharp slap with her broad tail and vanished into the lake. Ben and Nat watched wide-eyed as she rolled in a somersault beneath the surface, her tail the last thing to revolve and emerge shiny from the water. She repeated her performance several times, coming boldly up alongside the canoe, then swimming on, doing her best to lure us away from the lodge. Nat and Ben were thrilled to have heard the baby beavers.

"We'd better go," Nat urged, anxious to leave the mother beaver in peace, and we steered out of the cove and paddled on our way.

By far, the best place for us to observe wild animals was from the safety of our own front porch or from the kitchen window.

One day in May 1987, Jay was in Stewart getting the mail. As I peered out the kitchen window, a movement down by the stumphouse on the far side of the garden caught my eye. I saw a large black and white wolf making his way warily toward some moose ribs, which Jay had set there to attract game. Normally wolves are extremely elusive, and we saw their tracks far more frequently than the animals themselves. Observing the flesh-and-blood creatures always made me feel acutely alive. I called softly upstairs to Natalia, who had just gone to bed, "Nat, where' re the binoculars?"

Half asleep, she thought that I had asked for a "rocking horse," and in nightgown and bare feet she squinted her way down the stairs. However, as soon as I told her that there was a wolf in the garden she snapped to attention.

With adrenaline rushing, we studied him through the binoculars. Everything about the wolf was alert, from his coal-black nose to the tail that he kept tightly tucked between his powerful-looking legs. Frequently he tossed his head up and stared at the house. His eyes were intensified by a gray mask. His shoulders were white and shaggy, and his chest and hind end were black. He was about 120 pounds of bristling beauty.

"Wow!" Nat breathed.

Accompanying him was a large black raven, which synchronized its movements with that of the restless wolf. We could hear the snapping of moose ribs, which he ate while moving from one side to the other, peering anxiously to the right, then the left. Meanwhile the raven perched on a log close by, lending credence to the theory that wolves and ravens often work as a team. The raven flies far and wide and spots the food, then leads the wolf to it. The wolf in turn breaks up the goodies into small enough chunks for the raven.

Grabbing a quilt for Nat to wrap up in, we moved out onto the front porch for a better view. We sat spellbound and watched the wolf with binoculars for half an hour. He seemed somehow familiar with our clearing as he stood panting, surveying it. When Ben started to cry loudly from upstairs, the wolf didn't react. Nor did an outburst from the geese startle him. However, twice he became uneasy and began to lope off down the trail, his muscles taut, only to return to the ribs again. The evening air was chilly, and I told Nat that she should go to bed before she caught a cold.

"Just a few more minutes," she pleaded. She had never had the opportunity to observe a wolf with such leisure. Finally, Nat went reluctantly to bed. Alone, I walked out into the yard to get a closer look at him, and the creature's attention became riveted upon me. We stared intently at each other, and I thought of the "conversation of death" that some biologists believe happens telepathically between a wolf and its victim before it decides to make a kill. Then, abandoning his meal, the wolf loped away in a fluid motion, turning onto a trail that we had aptly dubbed "Wolf Way" several years before. Nat was still watching from the upstairs window. We could see the white and black bristle flowing between the bands of spruce and alder.

After the wolf's visit, all signs of the moose ribs vanished, but three days later a black bear ambled into the clearing and uncovered the mystery. From the porch I watched the bear approach along the river trail. Fresh out of hibernation, he was thin but his hide looked healthy. I called the rest of the family and they all emerged from the house to watch. Ben, at age one and a half, had a generous crop of blond hair, and two of his fingers were perpetually planted in his mouth while his index finger rested on one side of his nose. Seeing the bear, his sucking stopped and his eyes grew huge. Recently he had learned to "shoo" chickens, stretching his arms wide and following barefoot behind them, the way he'd seen Nat do. But sensing that a bear was out of his league, he hurried over and grabbed onto one of my legs. The bruin, on the other hand, didn't seem the least bit interested in us or the house. Instead it concentrated on digging up the moose bones that, we now realized, the wolf had returned to bury in several different spots. The first bunch the bear ate lying down, like a giant caterpillar, near the rhubarb patch. We tried to scare it off by ringing the triangle, but the noise didn't faze the shiny black beast. Instead it ended up hanging around for over an hour. Bears are poor eating in the spring, so shooting it was out of the question. It wasn't until Jay tore down the hill, firing ball bearings at it with a slingshot, that it finally sped, flat-footed and round-rumped, away.

At the beginning of June the wolf returned, inspecting the corner of the clearing that he was most familiar with. He was nervous, and after checking for his cache of bones, his shoulders hunched with disappointment, and he vanished into the woods again.

Later that day I raked up moose hair taken off a hide that Jay was tanning. With Ben in a pack on my back, I carried buckets of it down to spread over the asparagus as protection against frost. The day was cool and the tulips were folded together as neatly as turbans. As I worked my way along the row I could feel wolf eyes regarding me from the denseness of the surrounding forest. It made me recall a tale of adventure that Jay had told of his years alone in the bush—a story that would add an eerie dimension to our own children's memories of life in the woods and wild animals.

It had happened in February of Jay's third winter alone in the woods. Intent on living off the land as much as possible, he was keen on shooting a wolf for the hide, which would provide an excellent bedspread for the long and frigid winter nights.

One evening just before dark, Jay snowshoed around Desiré Lake with his husky, Spooky (our terrier was her namesake), at his heels. After returning to the cabin, he settled down to read until going to sleep. As it grew dark, Spooky, who was just outside the cabin, began barking and howling. Jay thought that there might be a moose coming around the edge of the lake and he called Spooky inside so that she wouldn't scare it off. A half hour later, when night had fallen, Jay heard wolves howling across the lake. Packs arrived often and would circle the lake, singing like a ragamuffin choir, harmonizing with spine-tingling notes that sometimes reached beyond the range of human hearing. Ordinarily Jay would sit by the window waiting for one to come into view, but that night he decided to go to them.

He pulled on his boots and coat, took his 22-250 rifle off the hook, left Spooky inside the cabin, and headed out onto the lake. By then a full moon had risen, illuminating the silver, snowy lake, but it didn't penetrate the darkness of timber along the shoreline.

When Jay got about 150 yards from the cabin, the wolf pack fell strangely silent. Jay had already decided that in order to lure a wolf over he would use himself as bait. He knew that the creatures often singled out and attacked the weak and sick, so he decided to feign injury. He performed a drunken stagger, falling to his knees every now and then and stumbling around in irregular circles. All the while that he was floundering about on the ice, he was working his way toward the opposite shore where he had last heard the wolves. After a while the pack recommenced its recitation, but this time it had an entirely different tone. Jay had never heard that combination of pitch and tempo before. They were working themselves into a frenzy, and it was all he could do to keep from turning tail and fleeing back to the safety of his cabin. He continued his charade and even lay still for five minutes after a mock fall. The savage voices reached a nerve-shattering crescendo, but still none of the wolves ventured onto the ice, which was covered with about a foot of snow. Jay rose and stumbled on for another hundred yards until a movement caught his eye. Three shadowy forms were moving silently and swiftly along the shore about three hundred yards to his right. Even though the moon cast dark shadows along the north end of the lake, he could count the three figures flowing between the shadows without a sound. In a flash they vanished behind a point of land. Jay continued staggering until he saw, out of the corner of his eye, three large wolves emerge from another point and begin running out across the lake between him and the still howling pack. Immediately Jay flopped down in a prone position; shaking, he aimed the rifle at the closest wolf. Suddenly all three wolves unexpectedly changed their course and started charging straight toward him. With his heart going wild in his chest, Jay pulled the trigger and jerked the gun upward in his excitement. With added terror he realized that the safety catch was still on! The wolves were still speeding toward him. Quickly releasing the catch, he took a deep breath and squeezed off a shot. One blast of the gun was all that he had time for. It brought the first wolf down in a tumble, and the other two seemed to vanish into thin air while the ones hidden in the shadows along the shore abruptly ceased howling.

Jay rose unsteadily and strode the distance to where the dying wolf lay. It had been hit square in the chest. Luckily one shot had been enough. In the moonlight he dragged the carcass across the ice to the cabin and left it outside the door for the night. No wails wafted out of the darkness of the surrounding woods.

When daylight came, Jay ventured back out onto the lake to inspect the tracks. Evidently at least ten wolves had been out on the ice when Jay fired. The pattern of footprints told a chilling story of how the wolves had been forming a circle, closing in on him. Then they all had dashed toward him, but at the sound of the gun they had turned and fled.

That same day Jay skinned his first wolf. It was a female. The hide itself measured six feet, seven inches from nose to tail tip, and the wolf weighed about 125 pounds. The night before he had been so excited that the animal hadn't felt very heavy, but when he hung it up to skin it, it was all that he could do raise it off the ground. The belly and legs were a cream color merging into buff near the shoulders. The rest was black tipped silver with a golden buff undertone. The jet-black claws measured one and a half inches in length. Jay took great pains not to cut the skin at all, and it took him most of the day to get the hide off the animal.

That night Spooky began barking again, and Jay ordered her inside. Soon after, the cry of a lone wolf rose into the darkness from a point not more than a quarter of a mile away. His howling contained the essence of mourning and as the minutes passed it grew louder. Jay had left the wolf carcass just outside his cabin door. Around 10 p.m. he went to bed, but the solo howling kept up and got louder for about an hour. Then all was still.

At 1 a.m. Jay was still awake. He was lying there with his eyes wide open, all alone at what seemed like the end of the earth, surrounded by silence. He was plagued with an uneasy feeling. All of a sudden the silence began filling up with what started as a low rumbling howl right outside his flimsy door. The howl rose steadily in volume and pitch until every window in the cabin was rattling. Overwhelmed with fear, Jay pulled the covers over his head and huddled there. After a few moments there was silence. Then he heard a loud woof. Then nothing.

The next morning Jay went outside and discovered an imprint of the wolf that had been sitting on the mat right outside the cabin door, beside the wolf carcass. He realized that the visitor had been her mate. He called the lonely one Beelzebub, and for many months afterwards Jay felt him following him through the woods. He would catch a glimpse of him now and then or discover the tracks later.

Natalia and Ben didn't understand their father's desire to shoot a wolf. Nor did I. However, through their father's story they gained an understanding of how wild these creatures are and a small illumination of their natural code of behavior.

Where it all begins—the lookout building in 1979. *Deanna Kawatski*

Our home in the Ningunsaw Valley. *Paul Bailey*

◀ Splitting wood.
Paul Bailey

▼Aerial view showing the house, the pond, and the garden in the foreground.
Paul Bailey

Nat and Ben peeling logs for the new barn. *Deanna Kawatski*

Wash day. *Paul Bailey*

Nat at the kitchen window. *Paul Bailey*

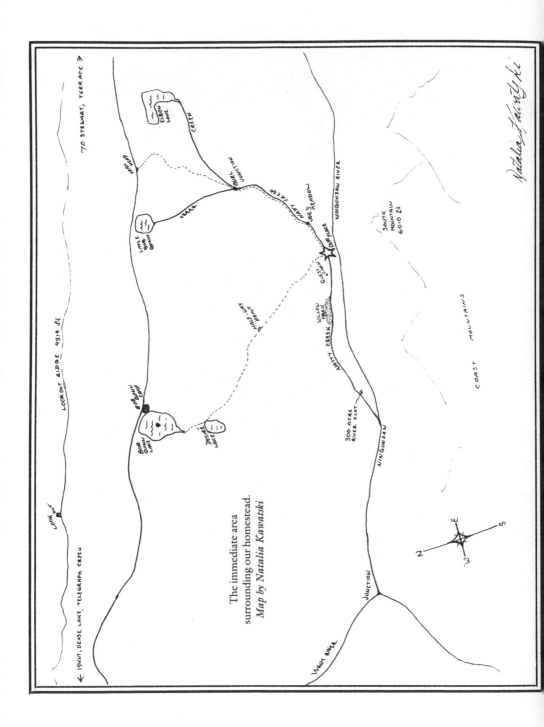

The immediate area
surrounding our homestead.
Map by Natalia Kawatski

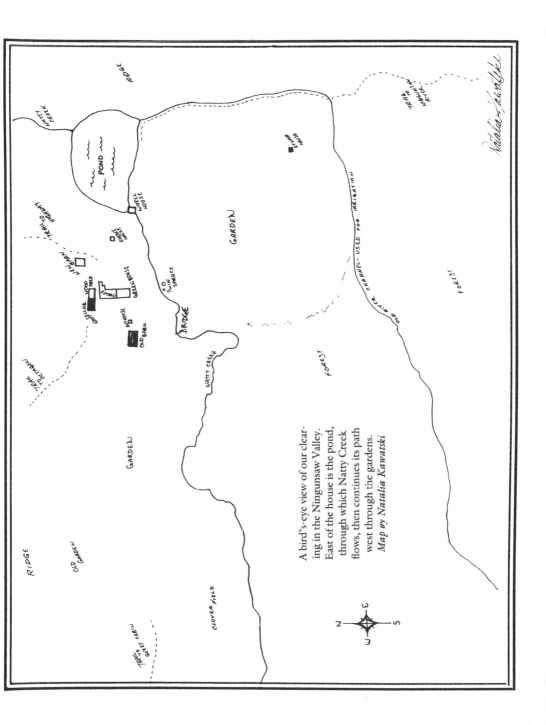

A bird's-eye view of our clearing in the Ningunsaw Valley. East of the house is the pond, through which Natty Creek flows, then continues its path west through the gardens.
Map by Natalia Kawatski

Chapter 7

Clothing, Cash, and an Automatic Wringer

WHEN I FIRST moved to the bush I quickly learned that as far as clothing was concerned, practicality came before fashion. My leather lace-up winter boots looked sporty in the shopping mall, but in the heavy, wet, coastal snow the leather grew soggy and had to be dried out for two days after each wearing. Freezing snow snuck between the laces, saturating my socks and transforming my ankles to a lobster hue.

When Natalia was an infant, Jay and I sewed her a luxurious fur coat to ensure that she didn't suffer frostbite when we were out hiking or snowshoeing. The coat was beaver with a wolverine hood, marten sleeves, and wolf's teeth for buttons. Natalia wore it her first two winters. One night we were skating back across Bob Quinn Lake. It was bitterly cold, and Nat was riding in a pack on Jay's back, wrapped in her cocoon of fur with her eyes peeking out from deep within the hood. As we glided along with our precious papoose, a full moon lit up the ghostly pyramids of surrounding mountains. I felt lucky to have my husband and child, and bewitched by the beauty around us.

Jay taught me how to sew skins, and beneath the halo of the kerosene lamp I would dampen the leather and wax the thread, methodically working from the skin side toward the fur side, taking great pains to pull the stitches tight while trying to keep them uniform. Over the years I managed to make several pairs of moccasins and mittens, using mostly domestic rabbit skins. When Nat was four I made her a pair of wolf slippers, and when she wore them she looked as though she had a baby porcupine on each foot.

I always felt more comfortable tapping out a tune on our antique Singer treadle sewing machine that Jay had owned when I moved to the bush. Even though I was used to working on electric machines, I soon adapted to the routine of spinning the wheel and jumping into the rocking rhythm with both feet. My first project was red flannelette nightshirts for the whole family. Jay's ended up too small, and being a restless sleeper, he soon burst through the yoke. Nat outgrew hers in a matter of months, and mine was the only one that lasted for years.

I made several outfits for Natalia, and once I recycled a pair of Jay's wool pants by making overalls for Nat out of them. Later Ben inherited them. There is something very satisfying about seeing your children dressed in garments into which your energy has been poured. However, more often than not it was patching and hemming jobs—uninspiring but necessary work—that took me to the sewing machine. With all the heavy labor Jay did, he was hardest on his clothes and they were patched and patched again. No garment was ever declared dead and fit only for the ragbag until daylight glared through its worn fibers and it was literally falling apart at the seams.

When I first arrived I knew how to crochet, but knitting was still a mystery to me. It didn't take long to figure out that knitting was the more practical craft and that the only sensible fiber to use was 100 percent wool because it wicks sweat away from the body and remains warm when wet. And animals don't have to be slaughtered in order to acquire it. My first knitting project took the form of a bulky sweater for Nat made from Icelandic wool. Later it was passed down to Ben. But for the most part my knitting took the shape of mittens and socks.

Despite my small efforts, most of our clothing was secondhand. My family at Shuswap Lake always sent used garments our way, as did Jay's mother in Wisconsin. And many friends thought of us when their drawers became too stuffed and they didn't have the heart to take their old favorites to the thrift shop or dump.

From age three to six, Natalia wore mainly dresses. On our hikes she would gracefully climb over windfalls while I kept a sharp eye out for the hem of her ankle-length dress, expecting her at any moment to snag it on a limb. Surprisingly, this never happened. Dainty even in gum boots, she'd prance ahead, her waist-length hair polished by the sunlight.

I'll never forget her as a five-year-old, dressed in a floor-length, long-sleeved, wine-colored dress. It was topped with a full red and white checkered apron. The dress had come from Nat's cousin, Annonay, who was dear to her heart. Each time we went to Shuswap Lake it was Annonay that Natty wanted most to see, and her cousin once came north with my mother on one of her visits. One winter night after supper, Natalia, decked out in this favorite dress, began to dance. First spinning like a whirling dervish, she then swooped and glided about the log cabin as agile and enraptured as a ballerina. Caught up in the joy of dancing, her face bore no trace of self-consciousness. I sat spellbound by her performance, her moment of pure inspiration. Sometimes, especially in winter, Nat and I still "kick up our heels," and Ben loves to join us too.

Nat's devotion to dresses lasted until the age of six when, on her trip to Shuswap Lake, she discovered that it was more common for girls to wear pants. Natalia returned to the bush sporting trousers, and I've rarely seen her in a dress since.

Nat and Ben both formed fierce affections for particular garments. When Natalia was two my sister gave us a red and white striped wool hat with a scarlet pompom swinging from the top. It had belonged to her youngest son, Isaac. Even though I knitted Nat hats and we received others from friends, Nat remained stubbornly devoted to what she referred to as her "candy cane" hat. From age two to seven she would seldom wear another. When she turned nine, I gently suggested that maybe she should give it to Ben now, but with much effort, she squeezed into it for another winter.

Ben became strongly attached to a neon green and purple sweatshirt with the words "Flower Power" emblazoned across the breast. His grandma Lorna had mailed it to him for his fourth birthday, and from then on, whenever a special celebration rolled around or he was simply in a festive mood, he'd proudly don his flower-power shirt. Around the same time he received a paper-bag crown at a birthday party in Stewart. Ben was so proud of the crown, which had his name printed across the front, that after he returned to the woods we seldom saw him without it. Each morning he'd carefully arrange it on his head, pulling it low so that it turned the tops of his ears down.

"Good morning, King Ben," I'd call from the kitchen as he descended the stairs, and he'd beam proudly.

One day, not long after he had become king, Ben decided to move out. Carefully he packed Lego, a library of Golden Books, and Benjy, his stuffed bunny, into a bag. When I asked him where he was going he replied matter-of-factly that he was moving down to the guest cabin, a five-minute walk across the garden and through the trees from the main house.

Then Ben's big dark eyes grew serious as he assured me in his bold voice, "You can come down and visit whenever you want. And when you come down I'll be wearing my flower-power shirt and my crown."

Since it was winter and the bears were hibernating, I let Ben venture over to the cabin on his own. However, when packing he had overlooked one item necessary for survival—food. Within an hour he was home again complaining that he was hungry, and moving out was quickly forgotten.

Like the flower-power shirt, some of our clothing came to us in the form of gifts. I took delight in wearing the navy, rhinestone-covered beret from Donna and the shimmering scarf from my sister-in-law Kerry, a bit of city glitter to brighten up my drab country-mouse wardrobe. And as I snuggled in the soft angora sweater from my mother, I was reminded of my love for my family at Shuswap Lake and my thoughts traveled across the miles to them.

In the spirit of conservation and recycling, we visited the Bob Quinn Lake Highways Camp dump now and then. It was surprising what people would throw away in their haste to leave the north. Nat and I made a trip in 1989. As we hiked the hefty seven miles to the dump site, located two miles north of the camp and just off the Stewart-Cassiar Highway, I reminded Nat that whatever we found we'd have to pack home. We were prepared to be choosy. Amidst the oozing oil jugs and ketchup bottles, rusted-out cars, rotting carpets, and moldy swollen manuals, we found several garbage bags of perfectly good clothes that were destined to be burned. Natalia and I pulled item after item—handmade sweaters, trousers, T-shirts, and even a sleeping bag—out of the bags. We gleefully displayed our finds, holding them high in the air for the other to see. By the time we set out for home, our pack sacks were bulging and our faces bore the expressions of delighted bargain hunters after a successful shopping spree.

Some items had to be purchased, such as underwear and footwear. We wore snowmobile boots—made with waterproof rubber bottoms and canvas or nylon tops, with removable felt liners—in winter, and for the rest of the seasons we wore running shoes and gum boots. I had never owned a pair of gum boots before moving to the bush, but before long the people in Stewart wouldn't have recognized me without them. Relatively cheap, they were ideal for our boggy trail. Ben and Nat wore them from the time they first learned to walk, and Ben received his first pair from a friend in Stewart at his baby shower, which was held before we left town, when he was less than one week old. She had searched the department store for the smallest pair she could find.

In order to purchase these essential items of apparel, some cash was necessary. Our annual income ranged between $3,000 and $5,000 and came from a variety of sources. Jay taught himself taxidermy, wood carving, and snowshoe making, and his expert work brought in cash regularly. Most of the sales were made privately, but he also displayed his wares in Stewart and at a truck stop thirty miles south.

The weather records we kept for the Atmospheric Environmental

Service brought in $820 annually. Furthermore, my income from magazine article writing helped keep us clad in gum boots and long johns.

Even though most of our cash was earned at home, in 1982 Jay accepted employment with B.C. Hydro. The job was offered to him shortly after we returned from a Christmas in Wisconsin. We flew back to Canada in January and arrived at our turnoff to find three feet of snow blocking the trail. It took us four exhausting hours on snowshoes to fight our way to our door, and when we finally got there, with Natalia vocalizing our misery in loud squawks, it was to find our black tomcat housebound. Due to the regular visits of a wolf to the yard, Tom hadn't left the house at all. Frozen to the floor were thirty piles to mark the month we'd been away. Upstairs in the frigid loft, every blanket plus our mattress was soaked in cat urine. Mercilessly the temperature plunged to minus 37°F and we had to huddle under coats and shawls on hard boards while cat and bedding were banned to the great outdoors. It was a rude awakening after a month of modern living!

Into this sorry state of affairs came John Bochard, a B.C. Hydro employee. He arrived in a helicopter in our garden and offered Jay a job as a sediment sampler beginning in May. The survey was being done at the insistence of environmentalists, as part of the feasibility studies that precede construction of large hydroelectric dams. After hearing the details, Jay agreed. We hoped that the survey would prove the river too silty to dam.

From May until the end of October, Jay made $55 a day seven days a week and spent three to four hours away from home, although the actual work took only about forty-five minutes. Each morning a helicopter alighted beside our garden as effortlessly as a spaceship, flattening the strawberries. Two-year-old Natalia and I often flew with Jay and thrilled at the freedom of whirling high above our house and gazing down upon it from the vantage point of ravens.

First we darted off toward the cableway on the Iskut River, descending deep into the five-hundred-foot canyon so that Jay could record the levels indicated by numbered metal plates, installed by rock climbers in five different spots and spaced a yard apart. The noise between the rock walls, which were less than seventy feet apart in places, was ferocious. The rotor tips were only ten feet from the vertical sides of the canyon, and we came eye to eye with Rocky Mountain goats, who balanced pertly on impossible rock ledges. Toward the end of May, baby goats were born in the Iskut Canyon, their sparkling white coats and dainty black hooves a joy to see as they shyly hid beneath their mother.

Leaving them, we dove so deep that the chopper skids hovered just above the angry café au lait–colored river that spit broken trees at us. Landing in snow, the pilot kept the chopper running, and Jay bounded over to the cableway, mounting the platform of the A-frame to which the heavy cable was attached. Sometimes he would take Nat and me. After hopping from the platform into the aluminum buggy, we held our breaths as he undid the rope break. It was quite a startling sensation to zip so suddenly out on a bouncy cable and dangle one hundred feet above the water in an open-topped metal box with a latticework floor.

At each stop two samples were taken. A glass bottle was placed into a brass device with a hinged opening, which was then lowered by a cable into the river, its descent timed with a stopwatch.

Next we flew to Forest Kerr Creek and then on to splendid More Valley. There we often spotted grizzlies and their cubs on the lush slide areas between timberline and mountaintops, where the spring greens prospered.

One perfectly blue afternoon when clear weather permitted us to fly to higher altitudes, the pilot sailed us up to ten thousand feet. It was like rising through the sky in a great glass elevator. In every direction the magnificent land was still locked in a sea of ice, with rows of rocky peaks like waves undulating toward the distant ocean.

By the time we set down in the garden again we had covered 120 miles. Jay and I were both opposed to mega-hydroelectric projects. We believed that it was tampering with nature on too huge a scale and were relieved when the plans were placed, at least temporarily, on the back burner. The job gave us the cash to buy the rotary tiller and the ski-doo. We also ordered a few select items of clothing from the Sears catalog. I fully realized that it would be folly to invest in too many clothes. The simple truth was that each garment carried with it a burden of responsibility, and the more we had the more I had to look after. For me this meant bending over a scrub board for hours on end and more mending jobs on the treadle machine.

Even after the diaper stage, active children tend to create a good deal of laundry, and it has never ceased to amaze me how quickly the dirty-clothes pile can grow from a single pair of socks straggled seedlike on the bottom of the laundry basket under the stairs to a bulging mushroom of grubby castoffs.

Until 1985, my routine was to move the laundry operation down to the creek in April and not retreat back indoors until the last golden leaves of September were spinning by on the current. The tubs were located across the yard at the base of a forty-foot hill. Hauling the laundry down and back up again to hang on the line didn't bother me. I much preferred scrubbing beneath an indigo dome of sky with the alder leaves rustling in the wind and yellow warblers and song sparrows serenading me from the nearby thicket. Clad in my ever reliable gum boots and standing calf-deep in rushing water, I even favored bending rhythmically in the drizzle to doing the task indoors in the dark back corner of the addition. Despite the work involved, Natalia showed streaks of enthusiasm for doing laundry. She would take the new agitator my mother had brought up from Nell in 1983 and pound with gusto, her feet leaving the floor with each stroke.

She would also join me at the creek to gingerly scrub her doll's clothes while I worked on hers and Jay's until my hands were red and aching. I was the easiest on clothing and had the least laundry, as I knew best the effort involved in getting it clean. Besides the scrub board and plunger I also had a sturdy hand wringer that Jay had bought from a mail-order catalog. I sometimes wore wool gloves inside rubber gloves to protect my hands from the icy bite of the creek, but more often than not I found them too awkward to work in and I'd pluck off both layers and toss them on the shore. When I couldn't endure the cruelty of the creek any longer, I'd yank them back on again.

One spring I was busy scrubbing baby clothes when I happened to glance up. Alarm seized me when I spotted a black bear sleeping on the lush hillside between me and the house. I began to shout in an effort to scare it away, but no matter how hard I yelled, the most the bear did in response was to lift its head off the soft growth and observe me with mild curiosity. Jay, hearing me holler, ran out into the yard with Natalia in his arms, and upon seeing my predicament he actually laughed! After a few minutes he grew serious and joined my efforts. The sound of an extra voice revived the bear, and, ever so casually, he rose and loped off down the trail.

After scrubbing for hours my back and buttocks would begin to stiffen, and when I couldn't bear bending over for another minute, I would stretch, take a great gulp of fresh air, and revel in the beauty around me—evergreen spires pointing upward against the distant snow-clad ridges and peaks.

In 1985, when Jay installed cold running water in the house, he set up the washtubs, complete with drains to take the gray water away. Doing the laundry indoors meant that I could heat water on the stove and thereby take some of the fight out of the creek water. Then in 1990, after eleven years of starting the fire and heating water in large kettles on the stove, we attached a cast-iron hot-water tank to the wood cookstove. Hot water from the tap seemed a genuine luxury.

At the same time Jay had been researching the possibility of introducing small-scale hydroelectricity into our lives. I pondered the changes this would bring and enthusiastically considered the possibility of one day owning a washing machine!

The inspiration for the construction of a waterwheel came from Denis, who was employed for a short spell at the local highways camp after he had quit his occupation as a diamond driller. His roguish appearance didn't conceal his kind heart or his keen sense of humor, and we quickly became friends. Craving the same kind of independent life-style that we enjoyed, Denis ventured alone seven miles up the Bell-Irving River, following game trails frequented by grizzly bears. On his own in the bush, Denis preferred to use his brain rather than his brawn, and his passion for electricity soon exceeded all else. He built a waterwheel even before constructing a house. When Jay went to visit him, Denis had a glowing electric light bulb hanging in a tree and a fan blowing the bugs away. Hence Jay's main sources of advice were books and Denis.

Most of the hard labor was in building the 6-foot-tall, 150-foot-wide earth-fill dam on Natty Creek. This work was done manually over several years using a homemade wheelbarrow and picks and shovels with handmade handles. The fill material was rock, sand, gravel, and clay mined from the hillside in front of the house. To make the wheelbarrow, Jay built a wooden box and attached it to the discarded front fork, wheel, and tire of a small dirt bike. Jay slaved season after season, moving tons of earth, in order to build the side of the dam up to the needed height. Two adjacent hillsides served as the other boundaries for the pond. When visitors, including Denis, showed up, they would often pitch in with picks and also helped haul the dirt.

To house the wheel, transmission, and generator, Jay assembled a ten-foot-square spruce log cabin on a cement foundation in 1988. That year he spent the snowbound months of February and March crafting a six-foot-diameter plywood wheel that he painted robin's-egg blue. It was a grand moment when the wheel was maneuvered through the back door, with some difficulty, and rolled down the hill. There it was mounted on a stainless-steel shaft in the wheelhouse. A square, twenty-foot-long, underground sluiceway built of rough spruce planking directed the water from the pond to the wheel, which operated a twelve-volt generator by belts, chains, and pulleys, most of which had been purchased through the Princess Auto mail-order catalog. A galvanized wire screen trapped any debris coming down the creek, and it had to be cleaned regularly with a hoe. This was most troublesome in autumn when the leaves were tumbling. A heavy electrical cable brought the power 150 feet to the storage batteries inside our house.

I'll never forget the moment in August 1988 when Jay trudged up our dusky hill with a heavy battery in one hand and an oblong light in the other. The glow from the wand was exceeded only by his fluorescent grin. It seemed almost too good to be true after ten long years of using kerosene, which was not only expensive and polluting but also dangerous. The sound of the waterwheel was not audible from the house, nor from the front yard. Halfway down the hill the trainlike rhythm began to be heard. The electrical system cost about $700 to set up, but the joy of our "enlightenment" couldn't be measured.

Two years later another revolutionary change came our way. On October 26, 1990, Fritz, a friend who lived near a native settlement called Iskut Village about sixty-five miles north, arrived with one-third of his washing machine strapped to a pack frame on his back. The rest he hauled in later. Fritz, a quiet and analytical type who was nothing short of a mechanical wizard, was originally from Delaware. He had married a native woman fourteen years earlier, and in 1990 he decided to move his family, which included eleven-year-old Gilbert and thirteen-year-old Julie, to a prize hillside meadow two miles from our homestead. There he built a home, complete with solar power. When Fritz and his family learned that I was fully responsible for the household laundry, they graciously decided to give me their own washing machine. Their system required that each individual take care of his or her own laundry. I marveled at their egalitarian method and looked anew at our own order. I was deeply touched by their generosity and fully appreciated what a momentous occasion it was for me. The arrival of the wringer washer brought an end to eleven years of hand-washing!

Several days later Jay and Fritz rigged up the machine so that it would function on our twelve-volt system. Once it was softly humming, we were like aborigines undergoing their first exposure to technology. We all hovered over it while the agitator swished the clothes

slowly back and forth, back and forth. Even though it was still necessary to fill and empty the machine manually and to guide the clothes
through the wringer, it saved me from the hard task of scrubbing each
item individually and the tedium of having to be so intimate with each
garment, especially every single sock. Occasionally, though, I'd miss
my many pretty and peaceful afternoons down by Natty Creek.

Chapter 8

Education
in the Woods

A T A DISTANCE of 120 geographical miles and 1,200 philosophical miles from the nearest public school, I enjoyed a minimum of conventional instruction when helping my children to evolve. The world was our schoolroom. In our simple life-style, opportunities for learning abounded.

For example, Ben and Nat learned through firsthand observation the intricacies of hatching geese in a homemade incubator. The process takes twenty-eight to thirty-four days and the eggs must be turned each day, just as the mother goose would do. The temperature of the box must be kept within a specific range, and the humidity must be maintained by the presence of a bowl of water. The eggs were laid by our own hen geese and were stolen from their nests by Jay. Geese, particularly when they are young, do not make the best mothers, so we stepped in. We've known them to waddle off to the pond, forgetting all about their eggs; some even step on and crush their goslings. The eggs were put into the incubator, which was a box constructed from local wood and outfitted with a piece of automobile glass for a window. For heat Jay installed a light bulb and also rigged up a thermometer so that we could gauge the temperature.

A month later, Natalia and Ben stared wide-eyed through the glass window in the incubator at the goose eggs and watched as the goslings hatched out, one by one. The young geese pecked their way very slowly around in a circle—a peck and small turn every hour or so until the shell was split into two pieces. At first the exposed goslings were wet, homely creatures with more pink skin than down visible. Spellbound, Nat and Ben watched as the goslings that were already hatched gabbed away to the beaks poking out of the shells, and the bills answered sassily. Before long the little creatures dried off and were transformed into balls of fluff. It was astonishing how, only hours later, they were running around preening, whistling, gossiping—being geese!

"How do they know how to do it?" Ben asked.

Our goose hen, Double Roll, was left to hatch four of her eggs on her own, but it turned out that one was rotten. Three goslings hatched, but the mother crushed two of them and Jay scooped up the lone survivor. Nat promptly began to comfort the lonely little creature. Sunny, as we soon came to call him, became imprinted on Nat and made a fuss whenever she put him down. He liked it best with his bill nestled in her hair or when he was riding inside her shirt. Sunny constantly nibbled at our hair and clothes, suckling warmth from our spirits and tweetling his sweet trills. Whenever Nat walked away from him he pattered after her on little nude pink feet, determined not to lose sight of "Mom." Despite how ornery the birds become in adulthood, Nat saw firsthand how a gosling would as readily attach itself to a human being as to another goose. The lesson continued when later it became evident that Sunny would never be accepted by the other geese, and Nat reluctantly agreed to give him away.

As for Ben, his counting ability certainly improved because he was constantly trying to keep track of how many eggs had hatched out. But most important, they saw with their own eyes the struggle and miracle of birth.

When Jay arrived home one spring with thirty thousand honeybees in a hive box strapped to his pack frame, they inspired much curiosity. With beekeeping, more knowledge is required than actual time spent tending them, and Jay had read many books, including the weighty *A to Z of Beekeeping*. He was a ready source for the many questions that cropped up while the kids and I observed the fascinating society of honeybees. We all took turns standing at the top of the ladder that led to the upper floor of the new barn, where the hive box was located. We watched the yellow bees, one after the other, soar out over the garden and clearing and then return to the hive box, their legs laden with pollen of different colors. When Jay (sometimes without the safety head net), lit the smoker, which sedated the insects somewhat, and withdrew the frames writhing with masses of bees, Nat and Ben would rush over for a closer look. They found it intriguing that these tiny creatures should be so temperamental and opinionated as to develop aversions to perfume, sweat, wool, black, white, and bright colors—which were but a few of their biases. Even though honeybees are docile by nature, the kids each sampled their wrath in the form of a sting. During their first year the honeybees wintered over successfully, and with any luck, we would learn how honey was extracted and sample its homegrown sweetness on bread made from wheat the children helped plant.

The various construction projects around our homestead were an education in themselves. In 1991 we began work on the new barn. The old barn beyond the outhouse remained conspicuously roofless, and even though we had housed the rabbits there for several years—beneath the protection of tarp-lined boards—we never felt secure having them so far away from the house. We decided to erect a small barn in the yard about thirty feet east of the house, well within earshot. We began work on the project while the snow was still on the ground. Jay cut the spruce and pine on the hillside above the yard and we all pulled the logs down the snowy slope with ropes. Jay worked at his usual intense pace and wasn't particularly patient with us as we struggled behind. Dressed in winter boots, old clothes, and work gloves, Natalia, Ben, and I sat astride the spruce and pine logs and peeled them with drawknives, the strips of bark landing on the solid crust of snow. I peeled eight of the one dozen legs, Ben and Nat each completed two. I helped Jay maneuver them into position, and once he had them notched tightly into place, they formed the base of the barn. For the upper section of the building Jay cut heavy beams. He assembled the sides and roof beams flat on the ground. The challenge was to erect the framework, and luckily our friend Christoph showed up in April and helped with this part of the operation. Using ropes and pulleys, we all held our breaths as the hefty beams were raised and the skeletal structure finally stood erect. Next Jay went to work on the roof. He hammered crosspieces onto the upper beams and covered them with balsam shakes, which he had hand-split in the front yard and nearby woods.

Jay filled in the space between the beams with a double wall of boards and also used some of the slabs that had been created when he cut the beams. These he lined with plastic. The children and I spent many days hiking through the woods gathering bulging sacks of moss with which to fill these pockets for insulation.

For over ten years the chickens had been housed in a tiny coop built in one corner of the woodshed. Now they were moved into the lower level of the new barn. We left the floor earthen so that they could scratch to their heart's content in winter. A ladder and trapdoor led to the upper floor, which was used for hay storage. Along the outer walls beneath the eaves Jay built rabbit cages, well out of reach of wild animals. Above this level was another substantial storage space. From conception to completion, Nat and Ben watched and helped with the evolution of the new barn.

The ability to read is the golden key to learning, and I encouraged this by reading to both children from the time they were born. Through my voice I tried to transmit my love of literature and language. Jay and I were both avid readers and the house was filled with books. We also borrowed books regularly from the Prince George Regional Library, five hundred miles south. These books were sent postage free in sturdy cloth sacks and we packed them in and out of the woods on our backs. With our infrequent trips for mail we weren't always able to return them on time, but the library staff was understanding. In addition, we had a steady flow of magazines into our mailbox. Natalia had a subscription to *Owl* magazine and Ben received *Chickadee* regularly. Both publications for children are put out by the Canadian Nature Federation and promote conservation and provide articles about animals and the natural wonders of our earth. All four of us also browsed through regular issues of *National Geographic, Harrowsmith, Country Journal, Canadian Gardening*, and *Equinox*.

One of our favorite times of the day was in the evening after chores were done, when Nat, Ben, and I would curl up together in my bed to hear a chapter or three of a book. In this fashion, over the years, we've been through countless adventures together. I read aloud the original unabridged editions of Mark Twain's *Adventures of Tom Sawyer* and *Huckleberry Finn*, all of the Laura Ingalls Wilder series, C. S. Lewis's *Narnia* series, *The Wizard of Earthsea* trilogy by Ursula LeGuin, *Charlotte's Web* and all the other children's books by E. B. White, *Anne of Green Gables* by L. M. Montgomery, *Pippi Longstocking* and other Astrid Lindgren books, *The Hobbit* and a good part of the Tolkien trilogy, and many more. I enjoyed reading these books as much as the kids loved hearing them.

From the beginning, Nat's reading level far exceeded that expected of her age group. I'll never forget the time when the children and I were traveling south to Shuswap Lake on a Greyhound bus. In the seat ahead of us two twelve-year-old girls, who had just completed the seventh grade, were discussing *Island of the Blue Dolphins* by Scott O'Dell, a book that they had recently been required to read. I glanced over at my seven-year-old daughter, who had read the same book the previous winter.

Nat was reading simple children's books on her own by the time she was four. Even so, I felt the need for some kind of guidelines for home instruction, so when Natalia was five I enrolled her in the B.C. government correspondence system. In two months she had completed her kindergarten course—designed for a year—and she had ample time to develop her own interests.

For six years, working an average of two hours a day, Natalia achieved top marks in the correspondence system, and she probably learned as much as she would have in a classroom in about one-third the time. Despite my doubts about the comprehensiveness of this program, I kept her in it because some of it was helpful. It provided a structure, and I knew that the alternative of devising my own agenda would have taken more time and energy than I had left after meeting all the demands of a homesteading existence. When an assignment came along that I felt was dull or unchallenging, we either eliminated it or replaced it with a project of choice. Sometimes an activity was assigned that Natalia responded to with enthusiasm. On one occasion, Nat spent all day working on a science project. She had to lie on a large piece of paper while I traced around her. Then she put in the respiratory, digestive, and circulatory systems. Next she painstakingly painted all the veins, arteries, and organs. The results were wonderful.

The principal of the correspondence program, Joe Vanderkwaak, and a teacher, Moira Sheridan, made annual visits to each student. My kids were the northernmost pupils in the district, and their papers and books traveled postage free back and forth between home and Terrace. Joe informed me that they had to walk farther to see us than anyone, and this alone made the kids feel special. The school created a link between our children and others who also lived in isolation and learned at home. And if Natalia continues to excel to the point where a B looks like a failure to her amidst all the A's, then scholarships may be available should she wish to go to college.

To facilitate their studies, Jay built both kids wooden desks with hinged lids. He did this despite his aversion to any program put out by the government and his firm belief that the kids would learn what they needed to know without any formal schooling. Ben's desk was constructed in 1990, and Jay put a padlock on it to ensure Ben's privacy.

Little Ben perpetually wore the key around his neck on a piece of green wool. He was more interested in the desk as a cache for his "treasures" than as a place to store his school supplies.

In September 1991 Ben was ready to begin first grade. Since home schooling was entirely my responsibility, I wondered how I would manage to find time for two students five years apart and on two radically different programs. About that time, the Ministry of Education had revolutionized the entire curriculum, and Ben was one of the first guinea pigs to try out the new Year 2000 program. I think Natalia would have thrived on it, but unfortunately she will be out of school before the revision of upper-level grades is complete. The new course is nongraded and aims at a more holistic approach to education, one in which the whole child is developed rather than simply the intellect. Of equal concern are physical, aesthetic, emotional, and social growth. The course revolves around a series of themes including friends, animals, insects, and so on, and then science, language arts, social studies, and art are brought into that arena. Each day the student is given two or three project choices rather than being forced through the only assignment available.

As is the case with many children, Nat and Ben knew how to print the letters of the alphabet long before they were required to do so. On sunny afternoons out by the river, they would take time out from splashing naked through the pools to pick up a river-polished stick and, with much effort and concentration, write their names in the fine black sand. Right after their own names and Mama and Papa, the word that they learned to spell was *love*.

Ben's program encouraged him to keep a journal, a practice that I've maintained for twenty years. As Ben sat at the wooden table in front of the rock wall clutching his pencil with purpose, his young face alert, I asked him what he would like to write or draw about for his first journal page. His big dark eyes surveyed the heavy ceiling and he mouthed his pencil thoughtfully. "Mmmm. I think I'll write about what happened tomorrow," he responded.

We all chuckled. He then drew a gorgeous spider sun with turquoise blue between its rays, a brown tree with a few yellow leaves, and some earth-colored ovals for spuds along the bottom. Next, with great effort, he printed, *Yesterday we dug potatoes.*

During another lesson I found Ben completely baffled by the concept of zero. He simply couldn't understand why there had to be a symbol for this if it meant nothing. Why not just start with one, which meant something? By the time he grasped it, I had reassessed my whole conception of zero. Indeed, home schooling is a learning experience for the instructor as well.

The program's project choices included singing, drama, nature walks, and numerous innovative art experiences. The fairy tale was one theme, and a project that Ben particularly enjoyed was going off in search of bits of nature that the imagination could weave into parts of a fairy world.

Clutching a bag, Ben set off ahead of me through the woods, intent on finding some fragments of a make-believe world. It was March and the earth was still largely snowbound. I plucked a piece of lichen called old man's beard from a tree and announced that I had found a fairy's shawl. Then Ben found bunchberry leaves for fairy wings, pussy willows for slippers, and a piece of dried cow parsnip for a wand. Before long the bag was bulging with little-people paraphernalia. Ben packed his treasures home and I helped him tape them to a large piece of paper and label them. Obviously the project didn't expand Ben's factual knowledge of the natural world, but it worked like poetry in that it presented him with a new way of seeing things. Later when he was asked to create his own fairy tale, he came up with the story of Bonaboe, a fairy who was born without wings.

Ben's vocabulary increased daily, and with sheer delight I watched his face brighten with the realization that with all the rhyming, repetition, and memorization he was actually learning to read. I feel fortunate to have been directly involved with this, unlike parents who lose their children to the public system and are always trying to reconnect with them by asking how school was and having to endure the bland answer, "Fine."

I felt sad, however, that our children couldn't regularly participate with groups of kids their own ages, and I knew they missed it. And so I made arrangements for them to experience public school from time to time. In fact, when Nat was in third grade, I took both children down to Shuswap Lake for a holiday while Jay stayed behind to look after the place. Natalia attended the North Shuswap elementary school for a full month. She reveled in rising early, catching the orange bus, and spending the day in the company of other girls her own age. What she didn't like was being forbidden to talk to them during class and how the authority of school followed her home at night like a dog nipping at her heels, hounding her to do homework in her few free hours. She also attended public school in Stewart now and then, but became increasingly reluctant to do so due to the crassness of certain boys who teased her about her boots and accused her of eating frog's legs because she lives in the woods. One obese boy, standing in the cloakroom one day, went so far as to say very loudly that he hoped "that dog" wasn't in his class. I tried to assure Nat that anyone who would say that to a perfect stranger must be suffering a lot of deep insecurities and pain. She understood, but it didn't take the sting of the comment away, and Nat had no desire to go back. She realized that these sporadic immersions would never make her part of the town community.

Ben also attended kindergarten in Stewart a few times and thoroughly enjoyed it. But since we didn't often stay in town for longer than three days at a stretch, these experiences were brief.

Throughout the years, Nat's chief complaint about her occasional attendance in public school was that she couldn't concentrate amid the classroom distractions. In the quiet of the woods, Natalia's artistic talent had begun evolving when she learned to hold a pencil at age two. By the time she was five, her drawing ability had surpassed mine. At a stage when most children were still drawing stick people, Nat's figures were surprisingly well proportioned. Not only did they show five fingers to a hand, but the fingers sported rings, the shoes had bows on them, and the facial expressions invariably made you look twice. For a long while girls were her main subject; their attire was elaborate, their hairstyles lovingly done. At the age of five she filled a poster-sized paper with drawings of at least forty different girls and women of all sizes and shapes, and it was amazing to see the interaction between the figures. Tall women swayed toward shorter ones like reeds in the wind. How did Natalia become so skilled with a pencil? Apart from the natural gift with which she entered the world, I attribute the development of her talent to long hours of concentrated effort in a natural setting.

Ben shared his father's interest in wood carving, and at the age of six he created his first piece—a flower with leaves at the base. Through this experience he learned the diverse nature of wood, noticing that in some places it was easy to make a clean cut, while in other spots the grain resisted the passage of his tool. He escaped with one small cut and the knowledge that it is best not to aim the carving tool at his own fingers.

In civilization there are constant diversions and distractions, including the most powerful one of all—television. Having grown up without television, Nat and Ben both had strong powers of concentration. Even as very small children, they were eager for me to read to them, even for hours at a time. We did listen to the radio whenever the reception was clear, and the Canadian Broadcasting Corporation had news coverage and some stimulating programs, including documentaries about the environment and social and historical figures; plays and satires; interviews with artists, authors, and musicians; and an abundance of classical music.

One winter Natalia and I waited eagerly each day over the course of two weeks for the next installment in a series dramatizing the story of Lillian Alling, a lonely Russian woman who, in the early 1900s, found herself in New York and desperately homesick. She set out and walked from New York to Alaska, following the Telegraph Line. Her ultimate

destination was her home in Russia. Nat listened in fascination, knowing that Lillian had passed within a few miles of our place, and that she
may have stopped by the same tumbledown lineman's cabin that we
stumbled upon while hiking the previous summer.

Chapter 9

A Natural Playground

A S FAR AS toys go, Natalia and Ben always loved to play with whatever was available. In summer, if a ball or Frisbee couldn't be found lying about the yard, a dried cow parsnip stalk made a good parasol or sword, depending on the mood, and a stroll down to the creek could bring forth a whole array of delights: a green rock glowing from the predominantly black pebble mosaic, a little gold toad, or an alder that leaned from the bank at an inviting angle, providing a perch halfway out over the water.

Manmade toys were given as gifts from friends and relatives, and throughout the years Jay crafted a few playthings, including a stick horse with a grizzly bear mane. The head turned out to be a touch on the heavy side, and two-year-old Nat developed a strong back maneuvering it around the yard. After Ben was born, Jay constructed a sturdy pine rocking horse with a black bear mane and tail. I remember vividly a bare-bummed Ben, less than two years old, vigorously inching it from one side of the house to the other. Later Jay built Ben a toy hip-roofed barn outfitted with hinged doors with tiny copper handles. Ben's hesitant fingers would open and close the doors as he moved the carved wooden animals back and forth between the imaginary corral and the shelter of the barn.

Often Nat and Ben entertained themselves with remnants of wood left over from various projects. These odd-sized blocks were decorated and became houses, a bakery, a bank, and a store—vital parts of the town that sprang up on the braided rug. However, once the kids were introduced to the building potential offered by Lego, the blocks were seldom taken from the box.

When Natalia was seven, Jay built her a large dollhouse. Even though at age two she loved to swing a pick and steer her little red wheelbarrow across the yard, and later was content to play with miniature trucks and cars in the sandbox outside the kitchen window, Nat also had a passion for dolls. At three, Natalia became attached to a Raggedy Anne doll and took her everywhere; she talked to her, read her stories, fed and scolded her, and even brought her friend with us to the potato patch.

At age two and a half, Ben formed a strong loyalty to "Benjy," a plump gray bunny that he received from Nell Morgan, a friend from the Shuswap Lake area. For years he wouldn't head to bed without hauling Benjy with him, and he'd sink into sleep with one sturdy arm wrapped tightly around him. Quite in contrast to the soft armful that Benjy provided, at age four Ben's favorite toy was "Berry," a tiny pink plastic bear that could be swallowed by an egg cup. The precious palm-sized toy frequently disappeared, and Nat and I spent much time helping a distraught Ben search for Berry. To make him easier to spot I crocheted him a tiny green and mauve hat and Nat sewed him a brown shirt. Ben wanted to leave Berry's coat open so that "everyone could see his nice shirt."

"Who's everyone?" I asked.

He replied matter-of-factly, "You. You and Natty."

The four of us celebrated the traditional holidays, including Christmas, Easter, birthdays, and Halloween, and excitement for the children preceded each special day by weeks. But for Ben, Christmas 1987 was a rather terrifying experience.

As soon as the fires were crackling that morning, Nat, at my insistence, threw on her housecoat and, with Ben in tow, scampered down the stairs to the stockings that hung on the rock wall. Nearby trembled the Christmas tree, adorned with unique ornaments that had been collected over the years—calico birds, straw baskets, and a red velvet elephant with gold sequins from India. Ben wore an old mauve and white hooded housecoat of Nat's, and he resembled a miniature troll.

Their wool socks each contained soap, a chocolate bar, a fluorescent marker, a toy car, and an iced gingerbread man peeking out of the top. While we were still upstairs, Nat had murmured that her stocking was likely to be full of gingerbread men because it was an annual ritual for us to make and decorate dozens of them.

Once the stockings were flattened by the work of eager fingers, I urged Nat and Ben to eat their breakfast of wild raspberry juice and fruit bread before opening the rest of the presents. It didn't bother me that we couldn't afford to spend a great deal of money on the kids. It had long been clear to me that numerous costly toys do not make for better play, and the depth of appreciation seems to diminish in direct proportion to the amount received. I even wondered if the ancient child, who played with a rag and bone doll, didn't have a more complex mind than the modern child who is given technologically advanced toys that do everything.

That Christmas, Natalia had been hoping for a Ken doll to accompany her Barbie doll to dances and restaurants. When she unwrapped the doll that I had ordered from a catalog, taking great pains not to tear the paper, she broke into an exuberant smile and her eyes shone, making it a special event for me as well.

For Ben, who was two years old at the time, I had selected a jack-in-the-box at the Odds and Ends store in Stewart. Nat, devoted to recycling wrapping paper, scolded him as he eagerly ripped the thrice-used paper into pieces. With fingers in mouth, he observed the red, white, and yellow box with a certain degree of skepticism mixed with pleasure. "See Ben?" I said, encouraging him to turn the red handle, which pumped out a hollow version of "Pop Goes the Weasel." Ben then turned it and cautiously ground out the tune himself. All was going well until the "pop" triggered the door to snap open, releasing a bobbing clown with black bowler hat, gaping red smile, and wiggly hands. Ben popped in unison, and when he landed his slippered feet sped as far as possible in the opposite direction, where he spun to stare wild-eyed at the monster box with the now benignly closed lid. All the while he fiendishly sucked consolation from the two fingers that were crammed even farther than usual into his mouth.

For days afterwards, Ben made quick-paced and wide detours around the jack-in-the-box, keeping his giant brown eyes fastened on it lest it should make any surprise moves. It wasn't until Natalia showed him how to keep one hand on the lid, so that the ugly clown would never again burst into his life, that he would venture to turn the handle.

At dinner that night, Ben proudly wore a new green sweat suit from his grandma Lorna. Jay was decked out in gray flannel pants and a blue corduroy shirt that I had made him, and Nat looked delightful in her pink printed dress from her Aunt Theresa in Wisconsin, blue tights, and pink hair bow. I wore a long, red, graceful dress from Turkey and had spent the day basting the turkey—purchased in Stewart and packed down the snow-covered trail—and playing with Nat and Ben.

With Christmas carols fading in and out on the radio, we set the table for our feast. Atop a green tablecloth from Jay's mom sat silver candles in holders that we had received as a wedding gift. All the dishes, from the giant platter down to the cups and saucers, matched; they were from a set that Jay had purchased from a catalog before I arrived. Nat scampered about filling the cream pitcher and sugar bowl and setting them out. Finally at 6 p.m. we sat down to a sumptuous meal of roast turkey, stuffing, lowbush cranberry sauce, and peas and carrots. We often roasted a goose at Christmas, and Ben asked first if the fat thing on the plate was a goose, and later if it was a wolf. Nat ate a whole drumstick and two thick slabs of white meat and a luscious bowl of carrot pudding with sauce for dessert. Later, clad in new nightgown from grandma Lorna, she pranced over and uttered, "I hope today wasn't all just a dream!"

I don't think it was simply the toys that impressed Natalia so but also the spirit of loving and caring that had gone into everything we had done all day.

Living three miles from the highway made hiking an integral part of our lives. We also hiked out of sheer love of the sport and tried to reach the top of one of the nearby mountains at least once each summer. I learned that when moving through the bush with children, it is best to simply enjoy being in the woods without being obsessed with a destination. Some of our mountain rambles would have tested the endurance of a hardy adult, let alone a child.

One day in August, weighted down with packs, including one containing our thirty-five-pound son toted obligingly by Jay, we scrambled over some impossibly steep mountainsides for the simple pleasure of reaching the beauty of the high country with its flower-strewn alpine meadows and panoramic view. Beneath our feet on the near-vertical slope was slip-away shale, moss, and lichen, and we clung to alder and poplar saplings to keep from whizzing back down the mountain. Following Jay's fast pace was an adventure in itself, and I'll never forget Natalia and me trailing after him down a rock face, clinging for dear life to anything, even gooseberry bushes, and leaning into the cold surface while vehicles on the Stewart-Cassiar Highway far below looked like Match-box cars.

On this trip we went prepared to spend the night on the mountaintop, over three thousand feet above our valley home. Wrestling with a labyrinth of fallen trees and devil's club, Natalia, then seven, reached her boiling point and spat out that she hated mountain climbing and never wanted to do it again.

But many hours later on top, as the fire crackled and we squatted in a circle around the glow and slurped sweetened tea, a smile spread across Natalia's face, reflecting our shared feeling of togetherness in that great lonely place. We didn't own any sophisticated camping gear, and darkness found the four of us packed like sardines in a pup tent beneath a single outstretched sleeping bag while the wind beat savagely against our fragile cocoon. In the morning the stars were still shining above a black peak that thrust up like a witch's hat in the east. After a breakfast of biscuits and hot chocolate we set out to explore the emerald alpine country. That evening we arrived home satisfied and bone-weary, with new memories to mull over during the long winter nights.

In winter our swimming hole became a skating rink. Nat had years of practice skating on the Ningunsaw River, but Ben's first time on skates was in 1990. I expected to have to bring a chair down the hill for him to hang on to, or that Nat and I would each have to take a side and usher his reluctant rag-doll body around the rink while his eyes bulged with fear and his skates buckled beneath him. But soon after Ben stood on skates he took off and was soon cutting circles around me.

Jay made snowshoes for all of us, using sturdy birch for frames and homemade moosehide lacing, and they permitted us easy passage through the snowy woods. Ben received his first pair at age four, and I would take him down the hill to the garden flat to practice. In red snow pants and jacket and red hand-me-down bomber hat, he would stride optimistically ahead of me until the moment when his shoes became mysteriously crossed, and he collided abruptly with the snow-cushioned land. He soon mastered the art of walking on webbed feet, and before long he was climbing mounds and hillocks with the sole intention of jumping off and landing square on his snowshoes.

Cross-country skiing was another sport that Natalia and Ben learned living in the woods. Nat's first set of skis was an old pair of mine that Jay cut down to size. After that we received hand-me-down skis from Donna when her boys outgrew them. I remember well what an ordeal it was the first few times I tried to help Natalia learn to ski. The more she fell the more outraged she became, until she finally ended up tummy down on the river flat yelling her head off, her ski-clad feet waving in the air above her and her mittened fists beating the ground. Despite the trials, it didn't take her long to catch on, and now she glides faster than I do and even downhill skis with ease. When Ben was learning he wore the perpetual white patch at the back of his snow pants with characteristic nonchalance.

In winter the Ningunsaw River became our highway and our skis squeaked out a curious tune as, exhaling ghostly puffs of breath, we carved peppermint stripes for miles down the flat while the sun glittered like scattered jewels across the snow. There was always some risk involved in river travel. In places, thin ice bridged the wild current, and breaking through would have meant being swept beneath it. The bitterly cold water would bring death by hypothermia in a matter of minutes.

In February of 1984, four-year-old Natalia traveled with Jay and me to the nearest hot springs on the Iskut River. To get there it was necessary to travel five miles west to the junction of the Ningunsaw and Iskut rivers and then follow the Iskut north for eleven miles. This river carried four times the volume of the Ningunsaw and was four times as fierce. Often its waters weren't frozen to a safe degree until February. Even then it was risky in places, but Jay was skilled at reading ice. Because the hot springs were inaccessible except by helicopter, very few people had ever seen them, and Jay was the first to reach them by river. On one blustery February day, with the help of our small Elan ski-doo, Jay broke a trail to the hot springs, dragging a length of black hose behind him to use to channel cooler water into the piping hot pool. Hours later he returned home with sulfurous smelling hair and an exuberant smile after a long immersion in hot water from deep within the earth.

Two days later, with the thermometer hovering around minus 18.5°C, we set out for the hot springs with Nat and me riding behind the snowmobile on the homemade sled. The sled was not much more than a foot across and about as secure as riding on a large dinner tray. With us on the sled, we also carried packs filled with extra wool garments, enough furs to keep our extremities from freezing, a cast-iron pan, cheese sandwiches, thermoses of tea, baked beans, sugar, salt, utensils, and a camera. We also carried a fire-starter kit composed of paper, shavings, kindling, and pitchy pine. Nat and I snuggled into furs and, giggling with excitement, we whizzed away. Snow flew up, stinging our faces, and I held Nat close as the sled whiplashed its way along the frozen surface. I kept my fur mittens pressed close to my nose and squinted with watering eyes at the restless ridges that descended the surrounding ivory mountains in a multitude of angles to the sparkling riverbed. Behind our sled we dragged forty feet of black hose that we would use to pipe cold water into the pool for a comfortable mix.

Five frigid miles and one hour later, Jay and I switched places and I maneuvered the machine upstream while Jay hunkered down on the sled with Nat. The sun ignited the western peaks and flooded the Iskut Valley with light. Otter tracks punctuated the white ribbon of river with exclamation marks of run, slide, run, slide, and I could imagine them gliding gleefully along on their bellies every few steps. I had to concentrate and use my body weight to balance the small ski-doo in the waist-deep snow. If the machine broke down, we would be in danger of freezing to death. Before long my fingers went numb from the cold and I switched places with Jay until he needed a break again.

When I wasn't driving I clung to the ropes at the sides of the sled and held Nat tightly between my knees. Our little girl was in fine spirits. Laughing, she joked, "Where are we? Are we in Hawaii? Are we in Yondon?"

In the east the silver ridges of mountains, riddled with the ancient trails of Rocky Mountain goats, rose and fell rhythmically. Above shone a blue sky with wisps of gold, while to the south hovered sparse clouds. With the worn orange tarp pulled up on either side to block the wind, the sled fishtailed its way down the lonely river toward natural untapped luxury. Blue ice-brows emerged inquiringly from the sides of sullen cliffs. In places on the banks the ice was piled like molten lava in peculiar shades of yellow and green. The velvety snow on top of the ice was embroidered with the tracks of mink, moose, wolverine, marten, beaver, and wolf.

Jay kept glancing back to make sure that Nat and I were okay. When he caught an eye he would smile and wave as the snowmobile bounded along the trail. His wolf fur hood framed his winter pallor. Then he'd scan the whiteness ahead, watching for any variation that indicated trouble. Before long we came to a stop. Ice had broken off the river's edges upstream and floated seaward, only to get locked together with other frozen chunks like pieces of a crystal puzzle. The pieces were jammed together and frozen into a patchwork of varying thicknesses and textures. The icy path that remained formed a bridge no more than three feet across, and beneath it churned the main channel of the Iskut River, its angry water, like green fingers, snatching at either edge as it galloped past.

Jay set his sights on where he wanted to go and roared across the perilous bridge. I held my breath and prayed until we were on the other side. The water was so close to the sled that I could easily have reached out and touched it. We came upon another such spot and successfully charged across it. Then Jay stopped the machine a safe distance from it. He grabbed the pot we had brought to make tea and I snatched a tin cup. Telling Nat to stay seated on the sled, we walked back, dipped our vessels into the icy river, and poured water onto the bridge. While we were soaking in the hot springs it would freeze into a more solid structure.

The last leg of the journey was through a narrow, high-walled stretch of river where the wind whipped us with snow beads. Two hours later we had driven as far as possible. Jay danced around, breathing onto his fingers, before he started to untie packs from the sled.

"The ride's over," he announced brightly. "Now we gotta hike!"

After setting the pack on his back, Jay hoisted Nat onto his shoulders. My mouth was tinged blue as I pulled on the other pack, but I bared a smile in spite of the cold. We walked as far as we could along the ever-dwindling lip of ice. Then we climbed straight up a bluff, using alders of varying strength to hoist ourselves higher.

Once on top it was a struggle through devil's club and brushy deadfalls. Our legs sunk thigh deep into the snow as we waded down the steep slope. Within a short time Jay and I were both carrying our heavy coats. At last we came, puffing, to the bottom of the hill with one last vertical twenty-foot drop to negotiate. I swung from a dead tree that leaned out from the hill until my feet encountered another limb to help break my fall, which ended in a slide down the steep bank. Jay swung Nat off his shoulders, and they both slid safely to the bottom.

We trudged on. Rounding a bend, we first smelled and then saw the sulfurous demon of steam, which rose like smoke from the springs. The bright green foliage of monkey flowers, growing in the vicinity of the hot springs, was startling against the black and white of winter. Nat was enchanted by it all. The bluffs of rock behind the steaming pools were deep green, salty white, rust, and bright orange, and they all streamed with boiling water. The dark sand around the springs was embellished with hoarfrost, which bloomed in feathery bouquets and coated the rocks with scales.

If Jay had not thought to bring the hose to channel cold water from a small pool nestled at the base of a black bluff, the water in the springs would have been hot enough to boil us. Yet with my teeth chattering from the cold, I huddled in my coat, unable to imagine getting undressed.

"Why not?" Jay asked cheerfully, and showed me how it was done by first peeling off his clothes and then laying them on the face of a huge rock out of reach of the steam.

Eager to enter the pool, Natalia jumped around in circles. I felt cruel undressing her in the icy air, but it proved to be a fleeting sentiment. She stepped gingerly into the water and Jay scooped her up. Naked except for their hats, they lavished in the warmth of the steamy pool, which apart from its black bluff backdrop was surrounded by the snowy shore.

With great reluctance I shed my clothes. My body was covered with goose bumps by the time I had inched my way into what felt at first like extremely hot water. Then I gratefully gave myself up to this wonderful immersion.

The three of us lounged about in the rich mineral warmth, far out of reach of help if trouble occurred. Each movement stirred up the thick layer of leaves, silt, and sand at the bottom, making the water so murky that we couldn't see our hands just beneath the surface. Even so, on a deeper level, it was a cleansing and completely invigorating experience.

"We're like three pigs wallowing in the mud!" Jay laughed.

Nat was in her glory, scooting around like a little tadpole, cooling off by playing on a brief exposed stretch of sand for short spells, then gliding into the warm pool again.

It didn't take us too long to realize that in our haste to get into the pool we had left our packs a good distance away on the snowy sand. There were four loads to carry, and Jay and I took turns making bare dashes across the snow while the cold jabbed mercilessly at our feet.

"I'm hungry," Natalia piped up, and with the hose Jay melted a patch of sand beside the pool for a place to build a fire. Submerged to the neck in water, with only my frost-covered head and one arm poking out, I grilled cheese sandwiches in the cast-iron pan, pushing them around with a fork. Heating up the beans was easy. I simply floated the plastic container in the pool until they reached the right temperature. We were starving after all the exertion, and the beans and sandwiches tasted especially delicious as we devoured them with only our heads and hands protruding from the sulfurous brew.

After lunch we busied ourselves dredging the bottom of the pool and building up the sides in the process. Nat's cheeks were bright red, and after flinging her hat off, her hair quickly became covered with an exquisite net of beaded frost, as was mine.

"You must be the fairy of the hot springs," I suggested, and Nat, in response, did a little water dance against the backdrop of the bluff.

We lingered in the pool for over three hours before reluctantly admitting that it was time to leave. After all, it would take more than four hours to get home, and we didn't want to cross ice bridges in the dark. I was the first to stand up, anxious to get the dreaded task of dressing over with. While we were wallowing the temperature had dropped at least three degrees. While Jay tugged on his wool pants I helped Nat into her clothes. I wore my mink cape over a heavy wool coat, and I pulled a bulky adult-sized wool sweater right over Nat's outer clothing.

Our bodies felt so heavy after the long soak that we could scarcely drag them back over the bluff. The sun had long since vanished from this narrow part of the river, and vivid green water rampaged past large rocks squatting at the edge of the current. In the center, boulders were topped by pale green ice caves that grew higher as the flow hollowed them out.

When we finally settled snugly back on the sled we all wore the glow of a very special experience. My hat was pulled low and my collar was up. I simply closed my eyes and hunt onto Nat with my knees and the ropes with my hands. It felt like a circus ride as the sled whipped wildly from side to side on the long ride home.

It was an excursion that Natalia never forgot, and through it she learned that the natural world manifests itself in diverse and startling ways, and that with energy and courage, it is possible to enter its magnificence.

Chapter 10

South Mountain Hike

"IF YOU TWO want to take off and do something on your own for a couple of days, Pierre and I wouldn't mind staying a little longer and looking after Nat and Ben and the place."

Parents and children need an occasional break from each other, especially those who live together in relative isolation, and Jane's offer sounded too good to pass up. We had first met petite, auburn-haired Jane Porter when she worked in the area as a geologist for B.C. Hydro in 1982. Now, in August 1987, she was accompanied by twenty-three-year-old geographer Pierre Friele. Both outdoor enthusiasts, they had just returned from a lengthy hike through Edziza Park, north of us, and their description of it made me yearn for the high country. Jay and I debated whether we should take this rare opportunity to go into Stewart and do some visiting or to go mountain climbing. The mountain won.

My times away from the children could have been counted on one hand. Nat and Ben were such an integral part of my life that I expected to feel a little lost without them. Still, I trusted our friends to take good care of our precious offspring. Natalia, then seven, and Jane got along very well. Two-year-old Ben, with his cap of shiny blond hair and large chestnut-brown eyes, was as round and wholesome as a bowl of porridge, and good-natured. One or even two nights away would be fine with Jane and Pierre, they assured me.

Often over the years, as I stood at the wood cookstove sweating and stirring, my eyes looked for relief toward the cool heights of the range on the far side of the Ningunsaw River. Ridges with permanent snow patches terminated at the dome of an unnamed peak that glittered with snow most of the year. The peak lay directly south of our homestead, and we called it simply South Mountain. We decided to make its summit our destination. We had been on the mountain one other time in 1982, but a helicopter had lifted us to an alpine meadow two thousand feet below its peak, thus eliminating most of the rigors of the journey. Our valley home lay at an elevation of fourteen hundred feet, and I was eager to climb, with my own steam, to the sixty-six-hundred-foot summit.

Packing was a hasty affair and, as we found out later, disastrously so. Pierre and Jane loaned us their sleeping bags, and we also took along our pup tent.

Natalia waved from the yard as we set out, and Ben, who was snug in Jane's arms, soberly watched us with two fingers planted in his mouth. In five minutes we broke out of the timber on the south side of our clearing and onto the Ningunsaw River flat. The wind, which had earlier been reverberating like a distant choir, had died and the sky was stunningly clear. On the far side of the jade-green, galloping river shone our destination. With packs positioned comfortably on our backs and dressed in jeans, T-shirts, and gum boots, we ambled a quarter of a mile upstream toward the slip-away bluffs from which loose gravel sporadically clattered.

Just before a beaver lodge, beneath elephantine cottonwoods whose full leaves exuded a sweet aroma, Jay stopped. He read the river with great concentration for a moment, then announced above the roar of the water, "This looks like a good place to cross here!" I hated fording the main channel of the river, and I guess my expression showed it. I had crossed side streams numerous times but had forded the main channel only once before. Even though I had done it without mishap, I was well aware that one false step could have sent me sailing off down the river. Jay, who was nearly always fearless, reminded me to face into the current so that it wouldn't drag me away. It would also be easier to maintain balance and footing that way.

The Ningunsaw River wasn't usually deep, but it was always swift and painfully cold. Spring runoff and heavy rains often transformed the river into a raging lunatic, and then there was no alternative but to stand back in awe of its power. Though the water was not at its wildest, I dreaded inching my way across the channel. Carefully choosing a piece of sturdy driftwood for a staff and removing my boots and socks, I fearfully stepped barefoot into the force and proceeded to sidestep my way across. I tried not to stare down at the water. I inched forward onto smooth round rocks shaped by eons of glacial water, planting my right foot firmly before bringing my left up alongside it. The river's icy grip reached up to my thighs, and by the time I got to the gravel bar on the opposite side where Jay was waiting, my feet were screaming for relief from the unforgiving cold. Safely on the other side, I tried not to think of doing it all over again on the way back. Yanking my socks and boots back on, and in my half-soaked pants, which I knew would dry on the long hike up the mountain, I scrambled after Jay.

We started into the coniferous forest following a healthy hissing creek that was crisscrossed with mossy logs. Jay had previously cut a trail adjacent to it for a mile or so and planned to eventually continue it to the top of South Mountain. In one place the creek was filled with a tangled logjam, an accumulation of tree carcasses driven downstream by the strong and erratic flow. Crossing on a large log that rested safely on both banks, we scampered up a forested slope and began to follow a ridge in the direction of the mountaintop.

We wound our way through the cathedral of dark, somber timber. The mossy terrain undulated with creek-laced gullies and high ridges. Luxurious moss carpeted the earth, rocks, fallen trees, and, in its enthusiasm, even climbed live hemlock. The north side of the mountain got less sunlight than the side of the valley where we lived, and once we left the river the growth was almost exclusively hemlock and moss, and the air was permeated with coastal dampness. In places, snow still lingered, and in other areas it seemed to have only recently departed. The river flat that we called home was a convergence for the coastal rain forest and the more northerly boreal woods. In contrast, the dark, silent forest at the base of South Mountain seemed somehow forgotten by the spirit of diversity, so that in autumn the few poplars that existed glowed like solitary lanterns among the vast evergreen. Its depths smelled like mushrooms and peace.

We had a four-mile maze of timber to maneuver our way through. Here and there Jay stopped and tied some flagging ribbon to a branch so that we could find our way back again. Eager to ascend to the open alpine country, we ignored complaining calf muscles and strained lungs as we hurried on our way.

Gradually the forest began to loosen its hold on the land and the wind-brushed alpine country bloomed before us. A flock of ptarmigan exploded with chicken-like cries into the air, infusing us with new energy. The emerald meadows on the mountainside two thousand feet below the summit were rippled with freshets, and in places the water formed terraced trickling pools that descended the mountain in neat steps. Around these crowded a chorus of wildflowers—purple monk's hood, sky-blue forget-me-nots, mauve fireweed, lupine, buttercups, and scarlet Indian paintbrush. I tiptoed through them as carefully as I would cross any flower garden. I thought of Nat and Ben and how much they would enjoy it up here, but then I remembered the river and knew that I would never want to pack them across it.

We soon picked out a camping spot—a level grassy patch on a larger quilt of moss and lichen over shale. It faced west, and the Iskut Valley far below was draped in its rich summer greens. Beyond that were the fluted edges of distant peaks. Home on the Ningunsaw was hidden from sight.

We had just built a small fire from the dead branches of a stunted alpine balsam when Jay asked, "Where are the forks and spoons? Where's the pot?" Bits of bracken clung to his beard as he rummaged through the pack. With dismay, as each fresh investigation produced none of the essential supplies, I realized that I had stacked them neatly on the floor and left them there.

Unable to hide his impatience, Jay demanded, "Tell me, how are we going to fix rice, eggs, and oatmeal when we don't even have a blasted pot?"

"Well, at least we have the metal cups," I replied meekly, bringing them forth from the canvas pocket.

Once we had a fire crackling we spent the next two hours cooking tiny courses of rice, eggs, and hot chocolate, with me rinsing the cups in a nearby stream between servings. We used our pocketknives for spoons, and despite my residing remorse, I could not suppress my amusement every time I glanced over at Jay consuming mouse-sized bites with grumpy resignation.

The end of summer was approaching and the nights were growing longer. Weary from the rigorous hike, we soon crawled into the orange pup tent for a comfortable sleep, cradled by steep peaks and covered by a canopy of stars.

The next morning we awoke to a calm sky the color of a robin's egg. While Jay started the fire I fetched water from a stream that trickled through a natural garden of monk's hood. The base of the stream was smooth shale lushly overhung with moss, dwarf blueberry, and low-bush cranberry. Soon the smell of coffee was drifting on the alpine air, and as we slurped it gratefully a blue grouse burst from a nearby tangle of balsam. Jay's eyes followed its flight, and he suggested that we walk around to the far side of the mountain and follow the ridge back. Even though my legs were tired from the hefty hike of the previous afternoon, I was eager to set out and explore the mountain, and also to climb to the summit, still two thousand feet above us. The air was completely still.

We piled most of our gear and left it there to pick up later. Donning our lightened packs, we set out through a medley of low vegetation. The wistful piping of a hermit thrust wafted up to us as we waded through knee-deep grass. Sporadic boulders were encrusted with lichen. The ground was riddled with lemming and marmot holes, surrounded by grass made lush from the residents' manure. The west side of the mountain prospered from a chorus of silver streams that cascaded down the flower-scattered moss. Delicate clumps of moss campion glowed from the ground. Suddenly at our feet we spotted a fat red lemming dashing for a shale cave. When Jay lifted up its rock roof, it scrambled for the cover of another one.

As we trudged on, a whole family of marmots, one after the other, ran across the sloping grass. They gleamed plump and silver in the sun, and when they stopped to perch on their haunches and sniff the air, through the binoculars we watched their large toothed mouths open and emit G-note warning whistles.

Arriving at a clump of cotton grass that looked to me like a flock of tropical birds, I stopped to gather a few of the soft tufts to take home for Nat and Ben. Across large snow patches that hugged the slope above us ran the surefooted tracks of a grizzly.

Finally, over four miles later, we reached the far side of the mountain, where I had never set foot before. Glaciers, like magnificent jewels, were set in the jagged teeth of peaks, which flowed in waves toward the distant ocean. Plunging deep between the stunning ice and rock ranges were green, time-pleated valleys, as hidden and mysterious as the dawn of life. There was enough beauty to feast on for several lifetimes, and I could have happily lingered, but Jay was anxious to push on to the top.

I flashed back on the first time that I had set foot on the summit in 1982. Jay's younger brothers, Julian and Jason, and their friend, Jim, were visiting from Wisconsin. Being from a comparatively flat state, they had little experience with mountains. It was the summer that Jay was working for B.C. Hydro, and one of the pilots offered to fly us all up to the top of South Mountain. Our three visitors got lifted first, and they explored until Jay, Nat, and I joined them later. When we arrived, a pearl-white sky hovered close to the moss and shale heights, and the men were nowhere in sight. They didn't respond to our calls, and we began to wonder if they had stumbled off a cliff or met a grizzly. Soon we spotted them sliding down a steep snow patch high above us.

We ate lunch beside a stream that waggled like a forked tongue directly out of the mouth of a glacier. Natalia, age two, in candy cane hat and red jacket, wandered happily around plucking forget-me-nots. Then the ascent to the summit began. It was an all-four-limbs affair up a near vertical slope composed largely of pieces of shale. Being the only one who wasn't carrying a pack, I scrambled first to the top, resting briefly only twice despite my protesting limbs. The air was conspicuously thinner than in the valley and I felt sorry for Jay, who had Nat in a pack on his back. When I pulled myself over the last lip and set foot on top of the ridge that snaked steeply into the distance toward the north and the Ningunsaw Valley, I was filled with vigor. It was good to be on my own for a few minutes. Sitting in a sheltered spot waiting for the rest of them, I put my hands on the rocks and moss and felt the primeval power of the mountain flow through them. I sensed its presence—so much greater than my own in size, life span, and wisdom— and felt myself, ever so briefly, merge with, become, the mountain.

Now, over five years later, beneath a turquoise sky, I toiled to the top with Jay, then walked the winding ridge line several miles to the summit. On either side of the narrow ledge, glaciers clung and plunged downward for two thousand feet. At the edge of a sheer precipice, I carefully leaned over and surveyed the depths, my belly swaying with the possibility of falling.

Perched on a rocky outcrop, we warmed our backs in the sun as we gazed far down into the Ningunsaw Valley. From that height our home all but vanished, its significance swallowed by the immensity of the land. As we ate our moose, cheese, and onion sandwiches, I wondered aloud how Nat and Ben were doing and scanned the diminutive clearing with binoculars for any signs of life. Besides a thread of smoke that rose from the elfin house, all was still. The only sounds were the bright whistles of marmots.

Continuing on our way, we stopped to enjoy the view once more, then began our descent. Before long, directly below us lay the largest permanent snow patch on that side of the mountain. In 1982 the snow had been soft enough to comfortably boot ski—that is, slide our way down most of the two thousand feet on the soles of our boots. I'll never forget Nat on Jay's back, the red pompom of her hat bouncing wildly, whizzing down the mountain at top speed. However, what Jay and I now encountered was a snow patch as hard packed as concrete, and sliding its eight-hundred-foot length would have been suicidal. Instead we decided to boot ski the near-vertical shale. We continued until farther down the mountain we encountered another large patch of snow. As we stood at the top of it Jay stroked his beard. "We'd best go around this, but then maybe . . . " Without warning and before I had a chance to protest, Jay squatted on his heels and, like greased lightning, whizzed one hundred feet to the bottom. My mouth dropped in disbelief as I found myself stranded alone at the top. "Come on!" Jay hollered.

"I'm scared!" I yelled.

"You chicken!" Jay chided.

Surveying the situation, I saw that in order to avoid the snow I would have to go about a mile out of my way. Ignoring the frantic beating of my heart, I descended the shale to a place to a few feet below. Then, gritting my teeth, I squatted and took off across the icy surface, doing my best to dig in with heels, hands, and bum. Still, I sped out of control, and I knew that at any moment I could spin off across the cement-hard surface and crash. I could feel the ice cutting into my fingers like splinters of glass as I tried with all my strength to break my speed. Luckily there was a lip at the far end of the snow that slowed me to a stop.

A little farther down we met more hard-packed snow, and once again Jay zipped away. This second spot was smaller but also faster, and it had no "safety lip" at the bottom, only sharp pieces of shale. Luckily Jay caught me and saved me from a rough collision.

Lower still was the alpine bench where we had spent the night, and we clambered down to it and began to pack up our camping gear. I did so reluctantly because I was already tired from hiking so many miles, and I would have preferred to sleep there another night and start out fresh in the morning. But when Jay asked me if I wanted a rest I stubbornly said, "No," unwilling to admit that I couldn't keep up with him. I was constantly trying, without success, to prove myself to him. After munching a few bilberries we started down the mountain, expecting that we would have plenty of time to make it home before dark.

My face was flushed as we began the arduous descent. I left the alpine country most regretfully, and it now felt suppressing to enter the forest again. At the timberline the trees grew out of an extremely steep, mossy slope, and with thumbs hooked in my pack straps, I edged my way down into the forest. Between the railings of trees and nearly directly below me I could see my husband moving quickly along. Near a boulder brooding beneath moss, I sank into a squatting position, my leg muscles too tired to go on. Suddenly my right knee twisted violently and I screamed out in pain. My leg went into agonizing spasms that knocked me flat on my behind. Jay stopped abruptly at the sound of my scream and lunged back up the slope.

"What's the matter?" he demanded.

"It's my knee!" I wailed.

"Quick," Jay urged, "straighten it out or you'll never walk off this mountain!" When the worst of the pain subsided I contemplated the four miles of rugged, near-vertical mountain that lay ahead. But what I found most alarming was that waiting at the bottom was the Ningunsaw River, with home and our children on the far side.

A knee injury abruptly alters one's perception of distances. Even a trip to the outhouse would have seemed a lengthy ordeal, and *this* predicament seemed like cruel punishment for my own stubbornness. Finding a strong dead branch nearby to use as a walking stick, I picked my way as carefully as I could down the slope. Each time I put any weight on my right leg it cried out in protest. With my pack on my back I limped through the dense hemlock that was permeated by the smell of the moss and lichen that had lain there for centuries. Reluctantly I stumbled along windfalls that lay like giant's legs above sinister pits of devil's club. My shirt was soaked with sweat and the pain was exceeded only by my anxiety about crossing the Ningunsaw River. What would my leg do when the current hit it? What if I was swept away and was unable to swim?

Jay located the trail of pink ribbons he had fastened to the hemlock on the way up, and we were able to follow the same ridge to the point where it dropped down to the creek that flowed between South Mountain and the next one. Limping through the creek's churning water, I wondered again how I was going to handle the river crossing. On the opposite side we got tangled up in a patch of devil's club while searching for the trail that Jay had hacked out two and a half years earlier. Finally we found it and I limped on.

The light was rapidly fading when we finally arrived, exhausted and dirty, at the river. The black sand was inlaid with fresh Canada goose tracks, and an evening wind rustled the cottonwood leaves. Ultimately what commanded my attention was the water, galloping like an untamed stallion into the descending darkness. In the evening the water level rose, and Jay decided that it would be safest to traverse downstream of where we had made the initial crossing. I dreaded entering the water, and would have preferred to camp where we were and deal with the problem in the morning. At the same time, I knew that this would be senseless, since overnight my leg would likely swell and stiffen to the point where I couldn't use it for days afterwards.

"We'll leave our boots on this time!" Jay shouted above the roar of the current. Then he grabbed my walking stick and told me to take his other hand so that I was walking upstream of him. With packs on our backs we soberly advanced into the wild mountain water. I felt fresh terror as the river grabbed my legs with its icy grip, its overwhelming power trying to wash me away. We were in the main channel and I could feel the rocks, like giant marbles, beneath my feet as the water rose higher and faster up my legs.

"Focus on the far shore! Don't look at the water!" Jay hollered above the thundering current. I did my best not to fasten my gaze to the hypnotic flow, but suddenly the water was above my waist. In a single motion my feet were swept out from under me and I was sucked past Jay. He too lost his footing and, with hands still joined, we were caught by the numbingly cold current and were bobbing like pieces of driftwood down the Ningunsaw River. Then the powerful flow yanked my hand out of Jay's, and for a long moment that I will never forget, I was certain that my life was over. Suddenly I thought of Natalia and Ben and I was filled with a sense of loss so immense that surely it would follow me into death.

The next moment Jay lunged and seized my pack, but the river snatched it off my back. Sprained knee forgotten, I used my last energy to twist around and grip the lower end of the pack's frame. Fortunately, we were being swept to the opposite shore, and in desperation, we fought our way to a patch of rock and sand that jutted, like salvation, out into the river. We scrambled for safety and rested only long enough to catch our breath. Then, dripping wet, our feet squishing inside our boots, we stumbled home through the darkened woods.

ONE MAY DAY in 1988, eight-year-old Natalia and two-year-old Ben were playing with dolls out in the yard. The songbirds had returned and the air was ripe with song. I listened through an open window while I kneaded bread. John O'Brien, an old friend of Jay's, and his buddy, Elwood, had spent the previous night. Years earlier, John had worked as a miner for the Grunduc Company near Stewart and had spent many of his weekends at Bob Quinn Lake, where he and Jay met. John and Elwood were now employed by the Cassiar Mine north of us. They had struck out down the river earlier in the day to hunt grizzly and weren't expected back at our place until late afternoon or evening. Early spring was the driest season, and passage through the woods was announced by a cracking and crunching, in contrast to other times of year when the soft, resilient, rain-soaked moss absorbed every footfall.

I heard the twist of the burl doorknob and Nat, dressed in blue polka dot skirt and matching blouse, appeared. Her large eyes shone from a face that was infused with the health that only fresh air and the woods can bring. She blurted out, "Mama, Papa is building a fire down past the garden. Benny and I want to go down and roast marshmallows! Can we?"

I thought it best to investigate the situation myself, and grabbing the bucket of rinsed and wrung diapers to be hung on the line, I proceeded outside with Nat on my heels. Ben was standing in the yard clutching Jamie Hardhead, his Cabbage Patch doll, and gazing beyond the garden to where Jay, armed with a rake, was burning off last year's dead grass. The circle of fire was sprawling out with an intensity that I mistrusted, the forked-tongue flames feasting in a frenzy upon a smorgasbord of oxygen and dried growth.

I shouted down, "Is everything okay?"

"No! Bring buckets!" his voice boomed back.

Dropping the diaper that I was about to pin on the line, I tore back into the house to seize any five-gallon buckets I could find. When I stepped back outside with the empty buckets, ready to race down the hill to fill them in the creek, Jay bellowed, "Bring a hose and screwdriver!" From the hill by the house I saw Jay charge across the garden, scoot over the log bridge, sprint downstream, and seize the weighty gasoline pump, fully intending to cart it three hundred feet to the scene of the fire. By then, scorching crimson flames were fleeing in every direction, even toward the edge of the forest and the truculent bark bases of several two-hundred-foot spruce. With panic gripping my chest, I grabbed the hose, bounded back inside, and reemerged with a screwdriver. Nat snatched the hose from me and, dressed in her finery, tore down the hill and across the garden, trailing the ebony snake. Bolting down the hill after her, I was just crossing the creek when I heard Jay bawl in desperation, "I've lost the plug to the pump! It's gone! We can't use it!"

Catching up to Nat, I took her by the shoulders and demanded that she go back up to the yard and stay there with Ben. Sensing the seriousness of the situation, Nat wasn't about to argue. She flew back up the hill, her face clenched with fear. Armed with buckets filled in Natty Creek, Jay and I bolted as fast as we could toward the fire, and as we did so the flames that had been licking fiendishly at the trunk of one giant spruce suddenly gained hold. A thousand scarlet tongues screamed in unison as they scaled the full height of the tree in a stunning blaze of color. Flames shot thirty feet above the glowing torch, launching sparks that sailed over two hundred feet to the base of the eastern hillside and ignited the grass there. Abruptly the wind rose and a bridge of flame traversed the space between the roaring torch and a neighboring tree. At that point I thought that all was lost. Natalia and Ben must have felt the same, because even through the deafening din of fire gone berserk I could hear their loud, pathetic sobs.

And there we were, feebly armed only with buckets to confront this formidable power. With these we feverishly scooped water out of the shallow former creek bed. Luckily, Jay had recently diverted some of the flow in that direction for irrigation. It would have been impossible to fight the fire if we'd had to carry buckets four hundred feet from the main creek.

Under the weight of the full five-gallon buckets, I struggled back to the heat of the battle. The smoke was so thick that I was choking on it, and tears were streaming down my face. I spotted a fresh trouble spot in the east end of the garden while in the midst of fighting a wicked patch of fire that was simultaneously working its way up four huge spruce. I felt that the hair was going to be singed off my head by the scorching heat as I flung bucket after bucket of water on the flames.

The fire devoured dead limbs, dry grass, stumps, logs, everything with furious gusto. I kept hoping that John and Elwood would return, but they were miles away, and at that time we had no way to summon help. I prayed that my bad knee wouldn't buckle, because Jay alone would have been defeated by the magnitude of the blaze. Our biggest fear was that it would turn into a full-fledged forest fire that would destroy not only our home and the river flat but forest for miles around. Whether we ourselves would escape was questionable. Natalia and Ben had heard us discuss the danger of forest fires, and judging from the howls wafting down from the hill, they thought that we would lose everything. Later Nat told me that the sparks were flying right around the house and over the chicken coop, and that the smoke was so dense that she could hardly see past the yard.

Meanwhile, in the thick of it, the smoke blinded me beyond a few feet ahead. My pants were soaked from sloshing water on them, and I was smeared with charcoal. My nostrils were filled with the stench of burning. Where's Jay? I kept wondering. It felt so futile to be flinging water on one small portion of the fire when it was impossible to see whether or not our efforts were in vain.

It took us two exhausting, terror-filled hours to triumph over the worst of it. When the flames finally began to subside, Nat told Ben to stay in the yard and she dashed down the hill armed with a rusty lard pail. Daintily she began to carry water to the smoking spots, and she also helped extinguish the fire on the east side, which was working its way menacingly toward a towering spruce.

The fact that we managed to put the fire out seemed like nothing short of a miracle. Once the danger had passed, Jay plugged the pump with a piece of wood, started it up, and soaked the vicinity. It wasn't until the panic had subsided that we realized how filthy we were. We were all saturated. There were holes in my gum boots and my socks were black from ash. Nat had a large black blob on the front of her wet blouse and skirt. Ben, who had also located a can and pitched in with the mop-up operation, bore the same charcoal insignia on the front of his Smurf shirt.

When John and Elwood returned at seven that evening, Jay was still hosing down the area. They couldn't believe how lucky we were. Later as Nat put on her pajamas she told me that she had dreamed two nights earlier that there was a forest fire all around us. I was greatly relieved that it had never got to that point, and the fact that we had triumphed over it added to my inner strength. I tucked Nat and Ben in with extra tenderness that evening, and when I finally crawled into bed and closed my eyes for a much needed sleep, my mind was filled with the images of gyrating flames.

Chapter 12

Ice

"**B**EN!" I SCREAMED frantically. It was early winter, and Natalia and I had been outside calling three-year-old Ben for half an hour. As always, my first concern was the still-unfrozen pond. I had dashed down to check the water, which reflected the snowy hillside, while Nat flew to search the woodshed. Ben had vanished once before, and after several panic-stricken moments we had discovered him upstairs, staring silently up at us, his nut-brown eyes calmly observing us from under a blond bowl cut, a volume of Mother Goose open across his sturdy lap. Yes, Ben had a bad habit of not answering when he was called.

As the surrounding forest, through which white ribbons of snow flowed, swelled in height and darkness, I was flooded with a feeling of utter helplessness. All the likely spots had been checked. While I was roaming the hill, still calling him through a throat gone hoarse, Natalia located him pulling the toboggan up the trail that led from the road to the house. Jay had gone up the trail earlier that day to cut windfalls that were blocking it. Ben had intended to follow him, but after trudging half a mile, he had given up and was returning home. The first thing I did when I saw him was to fly over and hug him like a mother bear. Then I let him know in no uncertain terms that his action was unacceptable, and that I had to know where he was at all times.

Natalia had never been inclined to do disappearing acts, nor was she as accident prone. Her cautious manner kept her free of the many hairy situations that Ben tumbled into. Long after he became steady on his feet, no matter how many times we warned him to be careful on the stairs, he'd regularly trip on a step and travel the remaining distance head first, or lose his footing and bumpty-bump the rest of the way down on his rear. It was painful for all of us to see him endure these spills, but remarkably, they resulted in next to no visible damage. Ben performed his most dramatic tumble when he was less than two years old. We had the unfinished upstairs of the addition railed off for safety's sake, and Ben, in overalls and undershirt, was gazing over the edge of the top board, which was at his shoulder height, at Jay, who was toiling away leveling the dirt floor eight feet below. Without any warning Ben suddenly leaned over and launched himself into the air. Nat and I were upstairs and we gasped as we saw him spinning through space. Miraculously he came to an abrupt halt on the back of his amazed father.

One of Ben's worst accidents occurred during his fifth winter. It was a Saturday night and Natalia, age ten, was filling the tub so that she and her brother could have a bath. A couple of inches of scalding water steamed in the bottom of the tub and the hot-water faucet was wide open. Ben was in a wild and jovial mood and quite unexpectedly, and fully clothed, he leaned over the edge of the tub and fell in! The near boiling water poured directly over the right side of his head. I snatched him, screeching to Jay, "Get the aloe!"

Splitting open the succulent leaves, which we grew indoors, we applied the healing egg-white-like liquid to the side of Ben's face. It was terrible to see the bright red patch rise up and to hear him cry nonstop for an hour. His right ear swelled to twice its normal size, and he was shaking. We kept him warm, and finally I got him calmed down enough to rest. I stayed beside him, comforting him, and holding more aloe against his ear.

Early next morning the first thing that Ben declared was, "Mom! My ear is all better now!" In actuality he had a second-degree burn that healed remarkably quickly. But the incident forced me to confront, not for the first time, the speed at which disaster could strike.

One of the drawbacks to living in isolation was that we were unaccustomed to being exposed to viruses, and when we did venture out to civilization we were sitting ducks for anything from the common cold to a terrible flu. I had seen to it that Nat and Ben were fully immunized, but overall, they had very little contact with doctors. So alien were these professionals to Natalia that at age three, when I took her to a doctor to see about a persistent sore at the corner of her mouth—we feared impetigo, but he assured me that it was only a cold sore—she said that she wished the doctor had been blue.

"Blue shirt?" I asked.

"No, blue skin," she replied.

Likewise, professional dental care was something we avoided because of expense, but I always insisted on good brushing practices and regularly inspected the children's teeth myself. Finally, when Natalia was eleven, I decided to have her teeth examined professionally. A dentist from Victoria was spending part of each month in Stewart, and Nat and I both traveled in for checkups. As I sat in the waiting room, Nat's slender form vanished into the inner recesses of the antiseptic-smelling office. Before long the dentist's kind face appeared at the door, and as he strode into the waiting room, I expected to be reprimanded for not bringing my daughter years earlier. On the contrary, he announced, "Your daughter has beautiful, perfect teeth." Having been subjected to regular torture by dentists as a child and having a mouth full of metal to attest to the fact, I was overjoyed to hear that my daughter, who had lived her life without fluoride or x-rays, had remained casually cavity free.

In any event, at home we had to actively practice prevention, and this was never more apparent than in January 1989, when avalanches blocked the highway from both directions.

That winter, as the heavy snow fell, I was deeply absorbed in a book called *The Survival of Civilization* by John D. Hamaker. The author presented a very convincing case for his theory that the planet was on the verge of another ice age. In the one-hundred-thousand-year cycle—ninety thousand years of ice followed by ten thousand years of warmer weather—we were, he theorized, at the end of the latter period. Hamaker claimed that even the greenhouse effect was a natural phenomenon preceding or marking the beginning of an ice age, but that human activity would speed up the advent of the next one. The author claimed that we must immediately do the glacier's work of remineralizing the soil or die from the oncoming ice age.

An unusually warm spell of weather in January in northwestern British Columbia was responsible for the softening of massive cornices on the nearby mountain peaks, which broke away and plunged toward the valleys in clouds of snow dust. The shrieks and thundering of avalanches were deafening as they tore their way down chutes loaded with windblown snow. Huge spruce and cottonwood were snapped like toothpicks, and trees and boulders added mass to the slides that charged at two hundred miles per hour.

One morning we shut down the waterwheel, which interfered with radio reception, to hear broadcasts of the avalanche activity from as far away as Seattle. We learned that avalanches obstructed Highway 37 between Meziadin Junction and Dease Lake and between Meziadin and Stewart, which meant that the highway was blocked both north and south of us. At least two motorists had had to be airlifted by helicopter off the Stewart-Cassiar Highway when they were caught between slides. A major slide had occurred in the Ningunsaw Pass, and more storm conditions were expected for the north coast. Stewart had twenty feet of snow in January. The wind had been getting increasingly strong, and my thoughts kept returning to *The Survival of Civilization*.

Within a few days the road north was open, with only one-lane traffic over parts of it, but our lonely trailhead was at the dead end of the southbound highway. With gloomy thoughts of an impending ice age and the knowledge that the avalanches spilling into the valley bottoms wouldn't be melted even by the following summer, I carefully perused our own situation. With the highway cut off, we would be stranded in the event of any emergencies. But barring the possibility of disaster, I realized that even if we were completely cut off from civilization, we had enough food to survive. Life simply wouldn't be as much fun without milk, margarine, and brown sugar. As it happened, we did run out of milk and were extremely low on chicken feed long before there was any indication that the road would be reopened.

The big news on the Canadian Broadcasting Corporation (CBC) station, broadcast from Vancouver, was an avalanche in the Ningunsaw Pass, only eight miles upstream from our home. It spanned the Stewart-Cassiar Highway and Ningunsaw River and was reported to be at least three hundred feet deep (later revised to sixty feet) and one thousand feet wide. There was an emergency meeting of the Department of Highways in Terrace, which determined that the size of the slide, measured on a scale of one to five, was rated four and a half. Furthermore, the record-cold Arctic air that was funneling south and holding most of British Columbia and a good part of Canada in its icy grip made it difficult for crews and equipment to work round the clock.

What we did have that winter that made the situation more cheerful for all of us was a neighbor. Richard, lean and energetic with a crown of rebellious brown hair and a perpetually curious mind, had struck out to find us after reading an article I wrote, "Living the Dream" in *Outdoor Canada* magazine. He arrived in September, and before long he had set himself up in a tiny cabin about half a mile away in the direction of the road—the hut originally built in 1980 by Joe, the ex-miner.

On February 1, Richard agreed to stay with Nat and Ben while Jay and I traveled six miles upstream to examine an avalanche that had plunged down just east of a narrow canyon on the Ningunsaw. Clinging to the sled behind the ski-doo, I finally arrived at the site with a bruised behind. Scanning the slide, we saw that the avalanche had shut off most of the main channel of the river, so that its waters were gradually building up into a glacier of pale jade-green ice that exhaled steam high into the air. Jay feared that the river would back up completely, and that when the warmer temperatures of spring came, the ice dam would burst, flooding our river flat. Still wallowing in Hamaker's theory, I remained doubtful that spring was going to arrive at all.

Gazing up beneath a powder-blue sky, we could see the fracture line from the avalanche glinting near the mountaintop at about six thousand feet. Everything below it in a wide swath was eradicated. The actual chute spanned two hundred feet, but from standing trees to standing trees the scar was five hundred feet wide. The white monster on the move had scraped up trees, rocks, and earth in passing. Jay and I ascended the avalanche chute and I took my mitts off to feel the frigid sides, which rose to a height of eight feet and were as smooth and hard as concrete. At random lay piles of enormous cement-like slabs that had ridden on the finer snow. As we climbed we came across several sets of wolverine tracks. These solitary creatures show up right after an avalanche, in search of carcasses.

Apart from having to step over one crevasse, we had no difficulty negotiating the chute. Scores of trees on either side of the direct path of the avalanche had been snapped like twigs by the fierce wind it created. Some were severed one-half or even three-quarters of the way up. Shattered trees stuck out of the mass of snow at all angles. The air was heavy with the odor of chewed-up trunks and limbs. Geometric pillars of snow lined the ridges of the irregular mass. I was freshly humbled by the power of nature and also amazed by the fact that this slide was puny compared to the avalanche that blocked the highway.

Northwestern British Columbia was still in the news, and the same day that we hiked the avalanche chute we heard a CBC Vancouver announcer interview the head of the Stikine highways district, who was staying at Bob Quinn camp. Word was that crews were building a snow road over the top of the avalanche and that the highway was still closed indefinitely. A full nine days after the closure, the Stewart-Cassiar Highway finally reopened to traffic.

On February 6, the whole family plus Richard went to view what some referred to as the biggest slide ever to come down on a British Columbia highway. Natalia and Ben were sandwiched between me— who endured the bumpiest position at the front of our little sled right behind the hitch—and Richard—who knelt, with agility, at the very back. We sped east along the frozen Ningunsaw River to a point five miles upstream where the river ran parallel with the Stewart-Cassiar Highway. In the canyon Jay briefly lost control on the ice and we spun in two full circles. Richard tumbled off but was unharmed. In spots we veered through the whipping branches of alder thickets. But despite minor scratches, we managed to travel the full eight miles to the main avalanche.

Leaving the sled and snowmobile at the river, we scaled about thirty feet of the massive mound of snow. The road had been cleared by then, and we all perched on a frozen mound and munched some fig bars that my mother had sent. Ben was more interested in watching the occasional truck go by than ogling at the magnitude of the slide.

On our way home again we all waved cheerfully to a passing pickup. We must have looked like an odd lot as we sped back down the river on the overloaded sled drawn by the ski-doo—the damaged hood of which had been replaced in 1987 with a half tin bathtub—driven by a bearded maniac in a raccoon hat. Even though we had chosen to live in isolation, for the sake of Natalia and Ben especially, I was relieved to see the highway open and to be reconnected with the outside world.

OFTEN I COULD sense the children craving contact with outsiders, and in our remote setting—where months could pass without a visitor—we all suffered from the crush of isolation from time to time. It concerned me that Nat and Ben had so little contact with kids their own ages, and I missed having other mothers close by to share my trials and joys with. The upshot was that we had a rare appreciation of our fellow humans.

Surprisingly, the summer of 1989 brought a bumper crop of guests. From May until October I seldom set the table for fewer than eight. At times I actually yearned for the old familiar loneliness.

Richard Thornton had renovated and seemed comfortably settled into Joe's dwarf cabin a half mile east of us, but he wasn't content to be a bachelor. He had lived alone in his tiny home for eight months when he came back from Terrace one afternoon with Solveig. It was white flower season, and the elderberries, Solomon's seal, cranberries, saskatoons, and wild strawberries all added their blooms to the festival of white. The tall, willowy craftswoman with long blond hair, wire glasses, calf-length flared skirt, and exaggerated arches in her long, tights-clad feet had picked Richard up while he was hitchhiking back to the Ningunsaw Valley after a shopping trip. Solveig had read the same article of mine, "Living the Dream," that had lured Richard to our doorstep, and it wasn't long before he convinced her that the bush was where she too belonged. It was also high bug season when Solveig arrived and she was horrified by the mosquitoes. Our cozy home was resonant with the communal song of our tormentors. A mob of them would accompany Richard and Solveig each time they visited. Solveig had two-year-old Tasha with her, a little charmer with blond ringlets and a bright dress. The other three children would follow once school was finished. Nat and Ben were thrilled.

A few days later, Freyja, Solveig's other daughter, arrived. She was nearly six, and the pale blue eyes that observed us from beneath the maroon beret spoke of her independence.

Only four days later, Julian, Jay's laid-back and amiable twenty-nine-year-old brother, shuffled in, fifty pounds overweight and puffing like a steam engine. Promptly, he became our couch potato in residence.

But the influx of people did not end there. One evening in early May, Philipp Pfefferkorn and Roy Gerstenberger arrived from Berlin. Our acquaintance with them had begun one year earlier when Philipp and Roy showed up at our door in the pouring rain. They were remotely connected to a German friend with whom I had shared an apartment in Berlin in 1974. Their dream was to venture out into the Canadian wilds, build a log cabin, and live there for a year. Roy, by profession an engineer, was tall and slender with thinning brown hair, deep-set dark eyes, a thoughtful manner, and a ready laugh. Philipp had a cap of straight blond hair, pale blue eyes, and the personality of an overgrown pup. He came from a wealthy family but earned his own living as a welder. Ben took a real shine to Philipp and was constantly seeking him out and hugging him. In truth we all liked them, and since they were so enchanted with the Ningunsaw Valley, Jay invited them to pursue their dream in close proximity to our homestead. We would charge them $8 a day for home-cooked meals and Jay would assist them with the construction of their cabin. This meant that after their stay we would have an additional building to use for a guest house or, I hoped, a writer's hut. They returned, one year later, ready to begin their adventure.

The day after they arrived they packed in their abundance of belongings that they had left at the highway. They had a heavy metal two-wheeled baggage mover, like the sort used in airports and train stations, and to this they fastened their huge metal trunks. Ben and Nat watched, awestruck, as our guests toiled, red-faced and sweating, into the yard with it. I doubted its efficiency on our boggy, erratic trail and noticed that they didn't use it after the first trip.

The two young men had also brought an exotic array of fancy foods. Hesitantly Nat and Ben bit into liverwurst, salami, German butter cheese, and Black Forest ham, and spat out the avocado.

Philipp and Roy chose a building site to the west about a quarter of a mile and a five-minute walk past our farthest garden. Neither of them had any experience with log building, but they had come prepared with books and the latest in tools. Jay helped them fell some of the trees, which they selected with great care so as not to alter the area too drastically. In rain gear and heavy winter coats to protect themselves from the insects, they peeled the logs and began to raise the cabin. Even though they sought out Jay's opinion as an experienced log builder, Philipp chose to argue with him over every bit of advice, and mealtime was often turned into debating hour. The site was hidden from view by a grove of stately spruce and balsam, but the whine of the chain saw, which they had brought with them from Germany, carried back to our house. Suddenly, for the first time in Ningunsaw history, we had neighbors on both sides.

Natalia and Ben reveled in all the excitement of having new people in our domain. When I first met the Berliners in 1988 I had expressed my desire for the children to learn German, and Philipp came equipped with books and tapes. As soon as their cabin was ready, Philipp promised to have Nat down regularly for classes, and in the meantime he used every opportunity to teach them phrases and vocabulary words. Ben, not yet three, pronounced the guttural words with the assurance of someone who was German in a past life. Our evenings were full of fun and laughter, and it was good to see the children relating to our newcomers.

With them the Germans had brought a radiophone in case of emergencies. Since we had electricity by then, they installed it in our house. Suddenly we had immediate access to the outside world and vice versa. But in order for anyone to be able to reach us, the radiophone had to be left on at all times, and its constant *beep beep beep* became obtrusive. Our enthusiasm was tempered with annoyance.

One night Nat, Philipp, and I strolled out to the Ningunsaw River and discovered it to be twice the size it had been two days earlier. Without warning it had been transformed into a great thundering mass of silty water spewing forth limbs, roots, and whole logs. Massive trees had been wrenched out of the earth, roots and all. One bore the silhouette of a hunched and sinister creature, which sped past, drove into a gravel bank, spun right around, collided with the shore again, and crashed into a grove of alders, seizing some to accompany it on its mad dance downstream. We were all humbled by the power displayed before us.

Then on June 17, just after breakfast, a red Vancouver Island Helicopter chopper circled over our clearing, then hovered low over the garden, blowing the plastic tomato covers awry and transporting the geese to the usual heights of honking hysteria. As four men from Stewart emerged, including the pilot, a policeman, and two avalanche technicians, the kids scrambled down the hill to meet them. They informed us that two days earlier a car carrying three eighty-year-old women traveling from Las Vegas to Alaska had left the road and landed upside down in the Ningunsaw River five miles upstream of our place. All three women were killed, but so far only two bodies had been retrieved. The men had searched the river without finding a trace of the third victim. Horrified, we promised to keep our eyes open for the remains of the last unfortunate woman.

Only four days later Jay, Nat, Ben, Julian, and I were wandering the riverbank when I noticed an unusually large flock of ravens swooping over to a sandbar and squawking loudly. I was convinced that the third body had been washed up on the island, which was separated from us by a rushing channel. Jay braved the current to investigate while Nat stood shuddering, as certain as I that it was the old woman. Fording the churning water, Jay shouted to us that we were right, it was a corpse. We all held our breaths before he delivered his final words, " . . . of a giant porcupine!"

By the end of June, Solveig's boys, Rune and Maru, had arrived, and on the first of July twelve of us sat down to dinner. I served sweet and sour moose, mashed potatoes, broccoli greens, salad, and for dessert, a chiffon birthday cake for Freyja. Nat and Ben were in their glory having four extra kids to play with, but I was already beginning to worry about them growing accustomed to having children next door and the void that would be left behind if they didn't stay. Still, it was a jolly evening, and I was relieved when Philipp and Roy insisted that since I had done all the cooking they would do all the dishes. As it was, preparing elaborate lunches and suppers as well as baking for the whole crew consumed a good portion of each day.

None of our visitors had ever baked bread before, and my kitchen turned into something of a bread-baking school. Philipp favored an unusual approach adopted from "Leben Aus Dem Lande," a back-to-the-land bible that he had toted along from Berlin. He was convinced that the best way to knead the dough was to pick it up and hurl it at the counter repeatedly with as much strength as he could muster. Ben would jump with each bang, which was audible all over the house and yard, and the Berliner was baffled when his bread was invariably flat and dense. We ran out of bread every second day, and one afternoon when Philipp cheerfully offered to replenish the supply he mistook icing sugar for white flour. Jay saved the day by converting the whole mess into ultra-sweet pancakes.

Throughout the spring Philipp had assured me that when his wife, Denise, showed up, she would help me with the cooking and the children. Philipp had married the twenty-four-year-old woman from Rio de Janeiro the previous winter.

Denise, a beautiful girl from Ipaneema, tripped through the back door on July 4, worn out from the three-mile hike. "I hate eensects!" she raved, and was horrified as well by the prospect of bears. She and Philipp had already seen three black bears on the road between the Terrace airport and the head of our trail. From upper-middle class Brazil, Denise was fluent in English, even though she was a bit rusty after spending two years in Berlin learning German. She had warm dark eyes, large perfect teeth, a dynamite figure, and was in the habit of dragging all her amazingly thick dark hair over to one side of her head, burying half her face alluringly in the process. It wasn't long before Natalia had adopted the same dramatic gesture.

Having noticed that we were short of pots and pans big enough to feed our crowd, Philipp had told Denise over the radiophone to bring some good German cookware. Denise had arrived in the Vancouver International Airport dressed in tight jeans with holes in the knees, high heels, bright red lipstick, hair swooped to one side, and clutching a frying pan big enough to simultaneously sizzle a dozen eggs in one hand and an iron pot large enough to make soup for thirty in the other. These proved indispensable.

Most of our guests had separate sleeping quarters. Philipp and Roy had not yet completed their cabin and, concerned about bear attacks, had pitched their tents on platforms that they built in trees about ten feet off the ground. Denise reluctantly followed her husband up the rickety ladder.

Despite her reservations about bugs and bears, Denise was enthralled with the wilderness. The kids and I took her on a walk around the loop path that circled the river flat. However, she complained that she couldn't see a path at all. Standing in the midst of the towering grass, delphinium, rose bushes, and columbine, blond Ben stood half submerged beside her and pointed stubbornly down at the trail, saying, "See? It's right there!"

Although she disliked cooking, Denise bravely took over in the kitchen for me on alternate days, and when we worked together I learned much about Brazil from her. She also spent time with the children, and I'll never forget the sound of her charming Portuguese accent as she red "Beeg Bird in China" to Ben. Nor will I ever forget when Denise contacted her mother in Rio de Janeiro by radiophone. While fluent Portuguese rolled off her tongue in triple time, Ben sat hushed on the step, spellbound by the mysterious rise and fall and varied rhythms of a language that made no sense to him at all.

By July 16 the lilies were flying their bright orange flags and there were nine of us sitting down to huge salads, fresh broccoli, beets, and greens. Our friend Denis D'Amour had arrived from Stewart, bringing with him a baby-blue turbine that he intended to rig up to give us additional electricity. He seemed surprised to walk in and find the extra people. Since his visits to our homestead were few and far between, he stayed for three weeks, sleeping scrunched on the narrow couch. On August 3, Julian left and took Denis with him, planning to drive him into Hyder and then to head to Smithers, where Julian had ambitions to soak in a tub and watch television. That night it was just Jay, the kids, and me sleeping in our house for the first time in fifty-four days!

Solveig and her children returned to civilization after living with Richard for a month. In Solveig's opinion, life was too short for bugs, children digging in the dirt floor, and cooking in the dingy cabin with the door closed against mosquitoes, sweating in front of the wood cookstove.

Late in the summer, Solveig returned with her daughters to visit Richard only to discover that he had vanished. A note tacked to a tree near the branch of the trail leading to Richard's cabin was all that remained. It began, "Hi gang," and went on to say that he had some "things to sort out," that he would be "back in a while," and to use what we could from the cabin. "See ya later" was his closing.

The next day I helped Solveig and the girls pack some of their belongings out. I had grown fond of the idea of having a woman and children next door, and as I hiked alone back down the trail, my prevailing mood was one of melancholy. Would my children never have regular playmates? I took consolation in the fact that Nat and Ben greatly enjoyed our older visitors. They tagged after them, and Nat spent half her time with her hair fastened up in a towel turban, a trick she had learned from Denise. She also began to worry about her weight—another trick she had learned from Denise—and I quizzed her, "Do you know why Solveig's kids are so skinny?"

"Why?" she frowned.

"Because they *work*!" Without further prompting Nat flew into a flurry of activity, which included washing the kitchen floor and tackling lunch for eight single-handedly. To cool off from the heat of the cook-stove she dipped in the pond with Denise. Ben, who had always hated getting his hair washed, decided to brave a shampoo. Standing naked, belly first and ankle deep in the water, he bent carefully, wetting only the crown of his head. Denise poured a blob of shampoo into his hand and, squinting, Ben lathered in the "magic stuff." Then sniffing boldly, he strode into the pond and bent again, rinsing only the topmost strands and leaving nests of soap at the back. Luckily, he liked Denise enough to allow her to finish the job.

On August 19, Christoph Bercher, a twenty-five-year-old horticulturist from West Germany, showed up for what turned out to be an eight-month stay. We had met the handsome outdoor enthusiast a year earlier when he had been touring northern British Columbia. He had spent a few days with us and had been intrigued by our life-style, and we had invited him back. It was a relief to have a visitor who was familiar with, and even enjoyed, garden work, since there were so many mouths to feed and more than enough labor for Jay and me. Then toward the end of August, Tobias Amon, a friend of Christoph's, appeared on our doorstep. They had worked together at a guiding camp at Chilco Lake. Toby came from near the Black Forest in Germany; he was very tall with a loose, friendly manner, black curly hair and beard, and elf-bright eyes. When he wasn't joking he was singing. Jay promptly put Chris and Toby to work expanding the root cellar.

As the end of August neared, we all went out to the river in the evening and had a farewell bonfire for Denise. She had been accepted into a course for hotel work and had to return to Berlin right away. I made a huge potato salad and Philipp had bought wieners, marshmallows, and potato chips in Stewart. These were rare treats for Nat and Ben.

Ben and the men sat on logs around the fire while Nat and I went to find Denise. We soon discovered her on a small island, separated from us by a deep river channel. Throughout her stay Denise had been wanting to cross to this oasis, and on the second to last night she found her courage. Without hesitation Nat ventured into the water and Denise met her near the other shore. I took my clothes off and followed. Feeling the familiar tug of water and its frigid grip, I remembered with a shudder the crossing that had nearly claimed my life.

The last sunlight of the day illuminated the spot where I emerged from the water to meet Denise and Nat. Denise was eager to show me some moose tracks she had found, and when Nat declared them old, she wanted to know how she could tell. Nat looked at her, astounded at such an obvious question. "Because they're weathered," she explained hastily to Denise. "They've been blown over and rained on. These leaves and twigs and other things wouldn't be in the prints if they hadn't been there a long time. They're dried out. And there's no loose sand kicked up behind the print."

We three girls strolled across the sand and rocks and finally sat down in a warm, shallow pool. Denise was buoyant with the discovery that life is everywhere, remarking that most people see only what is most obvious, like bears and moose. How true, Nat and I agreed.

With Nat in the middle, we held hands and traversed the channel again and joined the others. We feasted and sang a few ragged choruses, a hilarious cacophony of German and English. Slowly the stars blinked on and Ben and Nat were, as always, enchanted by the spectacle. They watched the great logs on the fire glowing with amber caves, licked by blue flames, showering sparks high into the air. At the edge of the river flat the giant cottonwoods glowed pale green in the firelight, offset by the black velvet star-studded sky.

In a way, our people-packed summer had been a saving grace, because it had taken our minds off the terrible destruction that was being unleashed against the virgin forest on the upper benches above our home. A week earlier Denise had toiled up the steep hill with Nat and me and gazed with shock and sadness at the ruins of what was once a vibrant virgin forest. Not too far away we watched a feller buncher, a machine that both cuts and piles trees, grasp its next trembling victim, hoist the severed birch as effortlessly as a toothpick, and lay it flat in a few motions. We wanted to cry out for the trees that could only stand passively and await their fate. Denise was genuinely appalled and stressed that it was every bit as bad as the destruction of the rain forests in Brazil.

On September 10 we were all sad to see Denise depart for Berlin. Six days later Tobias Amon left, intending to seek carpentry work near Vancouver. Then on September 23, as a pair of merganser ducks glided on the pond and golden birch leaves twirled earthward, my sister Donna, her husband Rick, and son Isaac showed up for a week-long stay. Rick helped Natalia build a lean-to on the hillside above the house, giving Donna and me time on our own. I had become less happy in my marriage, and Donna tried to help me see that it wasn't all my fault, as Jay had tried to convince me. I savored every minute of their visit, which passed all too quickly.

Our world had never been so full of the comings and goings of other people, and much energy was diverted toward temporary involvement in other people's lives. But it was becoming increasingly evident that Jay would rather spend time with any of the guests than with his own wife. His rejection stung me to the core. There were other sour notes. When Nat and I hiked to Richard's cabin to pick up the flour he had left behind, we found that the mice were already making a mess, and an air of dejection hung about the tiny domain. Aborted dreams.

Solveig, who was still hot on Richard's trail, made another trip out in hopes of finding him there, and also sent numerous letters to the Stewart post office, in care of general delivery.

By October, Philipp and Roy had moved into their cozy cabin. Hearing about the Canadian tradition of celebrating Halloween, they took it upon themselves to make it a special one for Natalia and Ben. Nat dressed as a tiger, in an orange and black skirt to which she attached a striped stocking for a tail. She fastened her hair with barrettes so that it resembled ears and drew red and brown stripes on her face. Nat had intended to dress Ben as a moldy mummy, but we were both disappointed when he fell asleep during supper.

Later Roy came over with the aid of his headlight to escort the lonely trick-or-treaters to his cabin. It was a dark, cloudy, and suitably eerie night as he led Natalia back down the hill and across the shadowy garden. Just before entering the swath of spruce and balsam that separated the garden from the tiny clearing around the cabin, Roy turned off his headlight and directed Nat to go the rest of the way herself. Here and there along the trail candles sizzled on stumps that, Nat told me later, were the color of tombstones. Stoically she hurried alone to the door of the darkened hut. Through the window Natalia could see the stub of a single candle glowing, and Roy arrived behind her and opened the door for her. The small, snug cabin had taken on creepy dimensions. Nat was told to sit on a stump while Roy seated himself on the only bench beside a dummy dressed in grubby overalls and a black sweater. It wore a pair of safety glasses on top of a black stocking cap that concealed everything but the eyes, which were outlined in red stitching. Even brave Nat was unnerved. Then the dummy began to release a series of miserable moans and groans. Finally Philipp, who was lying underneath the cabin with a microphone and a wire that was fed up through the floor to a speaker hidden inside the dummy, sensed that Natalia was getting too scared. He cut his act short and crawled out from beneath the cabin. When he opened the door and walked in dressed in a ghost costume, the familiar orange and once-white striped T-shirt gave him away. He also wore long johns over his jeans, a cruddy tea towel over his face, and flour and egg in his hair. The ghost strolled over and sat down at the table.

Still, strange noises persisted. Nat decided that Christoph must be hiding upstairs in the loft. Hoisting up the folds of her skirt, with her stocking tail swinging behind her, she ventured up the rough ladder to take a peek. All was still in the loft, but as she descended the ladder someone groaned horribly, "I want my stove!"

"It must be the ghost of Richard," Roy muttered, concealing a giggle. After Richard had been gone for several weeks, the Germans had moved his wood cookstove down to their place.

Just as Natalia set foot on the rough boards of the main level again, the trapdoor in the floor burst open. A creature in a mosquito head-net hung with old man's beard lichen, his body covered with thimbleberry leaves, sprang into the room. Nat screamed and in one leap landed on Philipp's lap. Without a doubt, it was a Halloween she wouldn't forget.

Finally in mid-November Solveig wrote to report that her efforts had not been in vain. She had found Richard! Following the clue that Richard had once worked at the Wildcat Café in Yellowknife in the Northwest Territories, she had traveled thousands of miles and tracked him down there. They were in love but had no intention of returning to the woods. Instead they would spend the winter in Quick, a tiny town about three hundred miles south of the Ningunsaw Valley.

Even by mid-November our chain of German visitors hadn't yet come to an end. As the Berlin wall was being torn down and the residents chipped away at it, danced on it, and threw flowers at Checkpoint Charlie, Karl Haus flew out of the city bound for our remote valley. Jay and Roy retrieved him from the Smithers airport in Roy and Philipp's rattletrap pickup truck, affectionately dubbed "Josephine." Karl was in his sixties with sparse gray hair, blue eyes behind dark frames, a wiry body, and a kind, almost apologetic manner. They led him through the woods by moonlight, but for him the hike was no hardship. Only the year before he had scaled Mount Matterhorn.

Though he stayed for only two weeks, Karl became, especially for Ben, like a grandfather. Indeed, it was a reciprocal relationship, because one of the biggest disappointments in Karl's life was the fact that he didn't yet have grandchildren. Karl bunked with Philipp and Roy in their little cabin, but each afternoon he would rise and, reaching for his coat and hat, announce, "I must go to Benny now." His English was limited, but Karl had brought with him a wordless game called Memory that involved matching nature pictures. About five dozen pictures were laid facedown. Then the player was permitted to turn two over; if they matched, he kept the pair and turned over two more. If not, they were turned over again. The challenge was to remember the location of the various butterflies, spiders, pigs, and so on. Children are, as a rule, very good at this, and Ben would skunk Karl every time. As the younger child, Ben was often left feeling that he knew less and was able to do less than anyone else in existence. Playing Memory with Karl was a great boost to his confidence, and I'm sure that Karl wouldn't have had it any other way. Karl also improved his English when he read to Ben, who would, without flinching, correct Karl's pronunciation.

In the years following Karl's visit, the children received a card and gift from him each Christmas. However, his tracks hadn't even vanished from the snowy trail before Frank Ehresmann appeared. A twenty-two-year-old photographer acquaintance of Philipp's with a nose misshapen by boxing, muscular legs, a confident air, and a kind spirit shining through his dark eyes, Frank arrived enraptured by the writings of Henry David Thoreau. Gripping a German edition of *Walden*, he expressed how much he longed to live "outside." In a singsong voice he proclaimed, "I can honestly say that I have absolutely no regrets about leaving Berlin."

Meanwhile the climate was showing its worst face to our foreign visitors. The mild, gray, drippy weather, which persisted all through the Christmas season, clashed irritably with their preconceived notion of a

Canadian winter. To make matters worse, tensions were increasing between Jay and me, and his behavior toward me was easily detected by our guests. No matter what I did he would criticize, mock, ignore, or scorn me. His temper was kept under control when others were present, but when he lost it he would shout at the children and me. Frank spoke to me one day when we were alone in the garden and told me how sorry he was that Jay acted so poorly; he wished he could do something, but he didn't understand it. As much as I appreciated the sympathy of outsiders, I also found their observations depressing and humiliating.

One day Jay was coming up the hill with a miserable expression on his face as I was going down. "I'm not happy," he told me, then went on to elaborate. "I've been living with you for ten years and I haven't learned a darn thing from you."

"That's your ignorance," I replied simply. This wasn't to proclaim myself a fountain of wisdom but rather to point out that if a person is open to learning, he can learn from anyone or anything. Then he exploded as he had on other rare occasions. I thought of my home and the valley that I loved so dearly and reasoned that maybe this was the price I had to pay for living in such a paradise. Despite everything, I loved Jay deeply and desperately wanted to work out our difficulties.

As winter advanced and the drab weather stubbornly persisted, Philipp and Roy became overpowered by nostalgia for their families and friends. They left for Berlin in the middle of January, four months short of their goal of spending one year in the Canadian wilderness. Frank lingered on in the cabin but he complained frequently about the weather and how much he missed boxing, running, cycling, and his friends back in Berlin. At the end of January, itching to experience a *real* winter, Frank departed for Alaska. That left only Christoph. When his visa expired in April he too vanished from our lives.

What did the children gain from this lengthy exposure to foreign guests? I think it broadened their understanding about other languages and cultures, and also taught them some of the dynamics of relating to a whole spectrum of personalities. More important, it showed them how essential cooperation is when functioning in a large group.

By far some of the most meaningful visits came from members of our own families. From the beginning my mother was the most faithful visitor, driving one thousand miles north to see us each year and bearing gifts of every description, including apples, prunes, and pears from her own trees, books and clothes for the kids, and once a weighty manual typewriter for me. Despite the brevity of her visits, which never exceeded six days, Natalia and Ben had the chance to get to know her.

In the fall of 1991, when Jay was surveying on the Iskut Road, Mom and Donna traveled north together. Jay, the children, and I were down harvesting potatoes in the evening when they appeared on the front porch, small figures in the distance, wondering whether we were home. I felt disappointed that I couldn't take time out to relax and enjoy their visit, but being good sports, they rolled up their sleeves and dove into the work. We lugged bucket after bucket of carrots up to the front porch. Due to the wet weather, gobs of soil clung to their roots, requiring us to wash each carrot individually before storing them away for the winter. The most leisurely part of their stay was a highbush cranberry–picking excursion through the nearby woods.

Due to distance, Grandma Mary, Jay's mother, had traveled up from Wisconsin only once, but Jay's brothers Jason and Jacob, as well as Julian, all ventured to our door. In August 1990, Jacob arrived from Virginia for Jay's first reunion with him in sixteen years. Dark eyed, with his fair, receding hair pulled back into a ponytail, Jacob, at age thirty-nine, was the chief gardener at the well-established Twin Oaks commune in Virginia. He plunged right into helping with the harvest. As a full-fledged member of the commune he had taken the obligatory vow of poverty, but he brought with him wealth in the form of the music he played on his recorder—an artistic skill that he shared with Natalia—and the spirit of his egalitarian community. On his bus trip north from Vancouver, Jacob had sewed puppets from a pair of his socks, and on a

Sunday afternoon he put on a puppet show about two frogs and a wizard. Having never been exposed to anything like it, Ben watched round-eyed, then clapped gleefully at the end of it.

During Jacob's visit, our pilot friend, Darrell, flew us all, including Spooky, up to the moss and shale heights of South Mountain. We spent the afternoon roaming the alpine meadows, with Nat and Ben racing down the slopes and flapping their arms in an attempt to fly. Mainly, though, Jacob's two weeks were spent helping us with the harvest. When he left to hitchhike two hundred miles south to where he could catch a Greyhound bus to Vancouver for his flight back to Richmond, Virginia, he said that he was taking a little of the Ningunsaw Valley back with him under his fingernails. We all wished that he could have stayed longer, especially with the onset of winter, which was a particularly lonely season.

The Simard family arrived on April 23, 1991, the same day that the trumpeter swan lingered on our pond. I was a little stunned to glance up from the quiche I was making for supper and see through the window an entire family of six flock into the yard. I immediately sent Natty to the root cellar for extra potatoes and carrots. Ursula Simard had written to me in response to an article of mine she had read, but they had gotten to our place earlier than expected. Nor was quiche suitable, since they didn't eat eggs, milk, or cheese. Meat and sweets were also on their list of forbidden foods. Her husband Michel was formerly a farmer in Quebec. He was thirty-nine years old and very spare, with dark hair and eyes, a trimmed beard, and clothing made of natural fibers. His daughters Arlene, eleven, and Karine, thirteen, were from his first marriage, and they were striking with their dancing dark eyes and long thick hair. Having grown up on an isolated farm in Quebec, they were painfully shy and remarkably wholesome. According to Ursula, they were fluent in English, but shyness kept them tongue-tied. All the females in the family wore calf-length dresses, long braids, and berets.

Ursula, thirty-five, whose enthusiasm for life was contagious, was from Germany originally but had spent five years in the United States.

Her six-year-old Esther, who had been born out of a former relationship, was a blond, freckled sprite who seldom stopped talking. She was a perfect companion for Ben. He spoke English to her and she babbled back in French, and somehow they understood each other enough to have great fun. The Simard family actually used three languages. Ursula spoke to seventeen-month-old Samuelle in German. The elfin girl, with a mere hint of hair, and cheeks made ruddy by a lifetime spent outdoors, was a joy to behold. It did my heart good to see Nat carrying her around and taking delight in her.

Michel and Ursula had been married for two and a half years, and apart from the prior winter, which had been spent in New Brunswick, they had been on the road the whole time. What was remarkable was that even with gas expenses, the family of six managed on $125 a week. But as they were quick to point out, they lived and ate "very simple." Their vegetarian diet was composed mainly of beans, potatoes, and grains. Breakfast was their main meal and they ate huge bowls of porridge with various whole grains and dried fruits.

With them was a friendly shaggy dog called Happy who guarded their camps. They preferred to live outside, without even the scanty protection of a tent. They used only sleeping bags, a tarp, and mosquito netting. We invited them to stay in our house or in the German cabin, as we referred to the cabin built by Philipp and Roy, but they preferred to set up camp in the unfinished new barn.

They stayed for four days, and while Ursula and Michel helped in the garden, Karine, Nat, and Arline split and piled wood. Ben, who couldn't get Esther's name straight and was constantly calling her Sylvester, dashed all over the clearing with her. Regularly they romped into the front yard to stir their "witches' brew," a concoction of sawdust, water, goose droppings, leaves, and other more obscure ingredients in a bucket.

The older girls were enchanting, and Nat adored having them for company. Even after a couple of days they were still too shy to speak much English, but their eyes spoke for them.

Combining work with pleasure, we all played Go Go Stop and Mother May I one afternoon on the freshly planted wheat field, which needed to be packed down. Then the girls were obliged to use English, and their Mother-may-I's were charming. They had had very little exposure to public school, but each day they faithfully sat down to the lessons chosen by their parents, and Nat worked on her correspondence lessons at the same time.

At dinner on the last night the Simards ventured to taste moose meat, along with mashed potatoes, green beans, and cabbage salad. As she forked the food in, I could hear little Esther quietly exclaiming over and over, "C'est bon! C'est bon!"

The Simards emanated love and happiness, and they left our clearing to journey on to Telegraph Creek and finally the Yukon in search of their own dream place in the woods.

Natalia and Ben waved wistfully as they vanished back down the trail. Like most of our visitors, the Simards had come and gone on foot. Over the years, guests arrived in a variety of ways, including by helicopter, mountain bike, all-terrain vehicle, dirt bike, horse, skis, and even once by boat on the Ningunsaw River. What each of these people had in common was that they enriched the children's lives—indeed all our lives—by adding yet another color to the tapestry of our understanding of humanity.

Chapter 14

Travels Beyond Home

O NE WINTER DAY when Ben was a baby, I stood on the snow-blown road while a savage wind rose to a blast that threatened to awake the bedrock. With my precious offspring, I faced a highway that meandered through the immensity of mountains and ice fields, and watched the only car in an hour sail on by. Finally, after an hour and a half, a middle-aged American tourist reluctantly stopped for us. Frowning, and without meeting my eye, the man from Los Angeles with gray wavy hair glumly told me to just throw my pack in the back. Some people are of the opinion that only bums hitchhike, and this attitude was etched in the man's profile. Motorists of this philosophical bent refrain from conversation because, judging by my mode of transportation, they're certain that if I opened my mouth, a gloomy story would emerge. When I quietly pointed out to this native of the city of lost angels that I couldn't possibly put my pack in the back because my pack contained a very sensitive Ben, the man gazed for the first time at my cargo. Dropping his mask of reserve, he and his wife and Ben and I had a warm visit in their Bronco all the way to Stewart. When they dropped us off the driver's face crinkled as he expressed how glad he was that he had picked us up. Ben waved from my back as they drove south toward California.

Even though traveling by thumb was unpredictable, with a complete absence of public transportation, we had no choice but to hitchhike up and down the remote Stewart-Cassiar Highway. This was the price we paid for not owning a car. Due to road conditions in this remote northwest corner, the life of a vehicle could be extremely short. Additionally, we would have had to park it three miles away from our house, and cars abandoned on the highway were soon stripped of all removable parts. So, between insurance, gas, and maintenance costs, we decided that owning a car simply wasn't worth it. And because someone always had to be home to tend the livestock, keep the weather records, and, in winter, stoke the fire so the canning and pipes wouldn't freeze, Jay and I usually traveled separately. Most often I took Natalia along and sometimes both children. Each time we all felt a little vulnerable, and Nat poked her thumb out most reluctantly. And though I disliked hitchhiking, and especially exposing my children to it, I also recognized how much my faith in humanity had grown through it. Most motorists' mouths gaped at the sight of anyone, especially with children, thumbing on such a lonely stretch of road.

Once, after a four-hour wait, we were picked up by a doctor from New York who was taking his nephew to Anchorage. The ten-year-old was the first black person that Natalia, age seven, had ever seen, and I had to nudge her to keep her from staring. The metropolitan doctor was fed up with his nephew, who was homesick and bored stiff with mountains and trees. The boy slouched, lost in the Narnia series, studiously ignoring the surrounding beauty and the local yokels who had suddenly invaded his space. However, he did emerge from his inner world long enough to give Nat a cookie. Nat was thrilled that the chocolate boy had given her a chocolate cookie.

When it came to rides, I learned that the most dependable motorists were the truck drivers, and they seemed to enjoy the company on their long hauls between Vancouver and Whitehorse and beyond. Some of the rigs were immense, and I would have to scale the sides of them, pushing Natalia ahead of me and wrestling my pack through the door, as the driver waited. It often felt as though we had just entered someone's living room, where warmth and conversation were waiting. And I had confidence in their driving skills because they spent more time behind the wheel than anywhere. I trusted them to pilot us through blizzards of dust in the summer, the suffocating powder sifting through the window cracks and settling between our teeth. Other vehicles stuttered past, far beneath the nose of the transport trucks. Motor homes and big trucks hurled out of the gritty clouds toward us. Winter was far worse. Glaring ice, blinding snow, frequent whiteouts, avalanches, and hundreds of logging trucks all made the highway a hair-raising obstacle course. I've seen pot-bellied, spider-legged truckers dancing around beside their rigs, unable to even stand on the glassy surface that they dared to drive on. Nat and I have waited patiently while seasoned truckers strapped on twenty sets of chains to make it up through Hannah Pass, the toughest climb between Meziadin Junction and Bob Quinn Lake. I was invariably obsessed with keeping track of our mitts and hats because frostbite could occur rapidly on the three-mile hike home.

In the spring of 1992, a trucker with tattoos of boa constrictors and roses on his beefy arms, thick gray hair waving past his shoulders, a bushy gray beard to his navel, and a deep love for the music of the Righteous Brothers blasted us with their sensational sweeps of emotion all the way to Meziadin Junction. Within the confines of his cab and sleeper he had four speakers planted. Natalia perched, cringing, on the bunk between two of them. The driver, who was traveling from Alaska to Washington to pick up fresh produce, would hold up his finger and say, "Listen to this." Then he'd crank the tape deck up to full volume. When Bill Medley's voice peaked, the trucker's powerful arm would go up, led by a stubborn index finger that pointed skyward with the ascending note. I found it a little curious that this big bruiser wore Chanel No. 5, and he offered me some, suggesting that I might not get many luxury items in the bush. I declined. Finally, with great relief, we hopped down from the truck at Meziadin Junction.

There was one occasion when I thanked my lucky stars that Natalia and Ben weren't with me. On this day in April, after hiking to the highway, one vehicle passed just as I emerged from the trees. I began to trudge south along the slippery, snow-streaked road. There was no traffic, and a clear-cut to the north was entombed in snow. Beyond the wind, only silence stretched out in a vast circle. I felt like I was the only person left in the world. Black branches scrawled against the sky. It was the ideal time for all the hard-luck hitchhiking stories I had ever heard to surface and haunt me. I recalled late evenings when Jay had stumbled in to report that he had had to walk fifteen miles.

It took one and a half hours to go a mile, because I wanted to give myself plenty of time to turn around and head home before dark in case I didn't get a ride. I was feeling a bit desperate when a grubby white shark of a convertible rumbled to a stop. My better judgment was giving me a good hard pinch even as I climbed into the backseat, but I knew that if I didn't get a ride now I wouldn't make it to Stewart before the stores closed. All too soon I was wondering if I would get there at all.

The somber, pale-faced driver with black wire eyeglass frames and a heavy mustache gunned the engine, and we rocketed down the road. Beside him was a slim native girl, and beside her was her Elvis Presley–like brother.

The instant the door slammed shut Elvis barked, "You married?"

"Very. With children," I replied.

"Aw, you're no fun!" he complained.

We had rumbled nearly to the bottom of Echo Lake Hill before I woke up to the fact that all, including the driver, were swigging wine out of their plastic cups. A gallon of rotgut sat conveniently at their feet.

"Do ya want some wine?" the woman asked with drunken cheer. I declined. It was 11 a.m.. I might have been better off had I accepted, because the road was parched and dust seeped through every crevice of the convertible. Much of it collected in the back, where I perched at the edge of my seat. To aggravate the situation, the window on the passenger side wouldn't roll up, and every time a vehicle passed I was unable to see or breathe. I was grateful for the scarf around my neck, in which I buried my nose. Each suffocating cloud prompted yet another coughing fit.

As soon as we got to where the Stewart-Cassiar Highway ran parallel with the Ningunsaw River, the brother ordered the driver to stop. "He wants to wash his hair in the creek," the sister hollered back to me, referring to the Ningunsaw River. Stumbling down a slip-away bank, he came close to falling into the current, and at that point it was difficult to think of reasons why this wouldn't be okay. While he was swaying and dunking his head in the stream, I asked the blasé driver if they were really in any shape to drive. He assured me that they were fine.

After the drunk had staggered back up the bank and fallen back into the car, all he could say was, "Man, that's a frigging cold creek!"

Despite the driver's words, I had little faith in his competence, and I was terrified the whole way to Meziadin Junction. I rubbed my worry stick, a piece of anxiety-polished driftwood from the Ningunsaw, and prayed. I kept thinking how crazy it was to hitchhike and how much I was putting myself at the mercy of strangers. The car sped so fast that it felt as though we were flying a little above the surface of the road. At the frequent appearance of an Arrow Transport truck with a balloon of dust billowing out behind it, the driver would slam on the brakes, so it seemed that we were either creeping or rocketing. Every couple of miles one of my companions would let loose with a, "Yee haaw!"

Elvis, who was drinking more than anyone, loudly proclaimed, "If I don't die today I'm gonna die tomorrow. It looks like a good day to die!" I clenched my teeth.

That the driver could see at all through his dust-caked glasses was doubtful. Now and then he would remove them and pass them to his woman to clean, and moments later she would hand them back, smeared. As the surroundings passed in a blur, we all became coated with dust, and before long we each appeared to have aged by about ten years. The dust landing on Elvis's wet head had turned to paste. His hair had turned a mossy gray and was stuck to his head like batter to a bowl. Just after announcing, "I haven't slept for a week! Been partying!" he passed out. Good riddance, I thought.

Thirty miles south, around a hairpin turn that truckers referred to as

"Suicide Corner," we came to an area freshly devastated by logging. The drive to town had once been through a lush corridor of green. Now the remains of the gutted forest lay there for the shocked scrutiny of the ever-increasing chain of tourists traveling through.

Relief swept over me when we screeched to a halt at Meziadin Junction. However, when I tried to get out, Elvis was too drunk to move. Reluctantly the driver crawled out so that I could escape from his side. I thanked them, and as they gunned it south toward Prince George, I wondered if they would make it.

Despite the dangers, trips out now and then were essential for all of us. In 1987, Jay hitchhiked thousands of miles to Wisconsin with seven-year-old Natalia, leaving me at home with an infant son. It wasn't really fear I felt at the prospect of being alone for two weeks. It was more a feeling of humility and being at the mercy of whatever forces chose to play havoc with my peace. As it was, a wolf came and went, but for the most part, I was left to weed the sprawling garden beneath a hawk-spiraled sky, beside a trickling creek, and to retreat inside at night and check the doors twice before mounting the stairs and nestling in bed with my baby for the whole bright night.

When Nat finally returned, her eyes held a new measure of maturity as she told remarkable stories about the sandstorm that had blackened the prairie as they passed through. She described hanging on to a telephone pole to keep from being blown away. And in the black storm hung the gloomy gossamer of tent caterpillars. In a whirlwind two weeks she had traversed a good part of the continent and attended her cousin's wedding; then she and Jay had driven home with Grandma Mary, Aunt Baryb, and cousin Caleb, who had come to visit for a few days.

Both Nat and Ben were very keen on trips out. Mainly we went to Stewart for mail, shopping, and visiting, and this happened about once every three months. My friends all had children, and they would play while Pat, Janet, Karen, and I shared experiences, recipes, and insights.

As distant as my town friends were, they were still a vital part of my northern existence, and I loved them dearly.

On March 6, 1989, when Natalia was nine and Ben was four, Jay returned from Stewart with Karen and Mike's well-worn pickup truck. He had borrowed it for a family trip to the Suskwa Valley, about a hundred crow miles south of us, to visit friends for a few days. We left the next morning in the freshly falling snow. Driving was treacherous, with a slick surface and high snow walls lining either side of the highway, making it impossible to escape if a logging truck suddenly veered over into the wrong lane. It was a black and white day. Flakes were falling from a white sky and piling up on a black and white ground.

I kept thinking that driving conditions were almost as bad as the last time I had been out with Jay. Then Richard had stayed with Natalia and Ben while Jay and I hitchhiked to town to attend a Halloween dance. It was the first time we had done this in nine years of marriage. The next morning a few cars passed by as we stood in the pouring rain outside Stewart thumbing a ride home. I was wearing my red beret and feeling a little wrung out after masquerading as a Twisted Sister, along with Pat and Janet, the night before. Jay had dressed as a faceless bureaucrat. Since we hadn't brought rain gear, he had outfitted me in a yellow garbage bag, and I felt as though I was still in costume.

Before long, Ian Macleod, owner of the King Edward Hotel and the ex-mayor, picked us up and said that he would gladly take us as far as Meziadin Lake. Toward Bear Pass the rain turned to snow, and soon the road was coated with a thick layer of slush. As Ian swerved out to pass a small car, Jay regarded the flat flakes spinning toward the windshield and said, "Beautiful, eh? Beautiful and treacherous!"

Ian, applying the brakes, went into a skid and lost control. The pickup truck fishtailed wildly from one side of the road to the other as he fought to regain command. Suddenly we were spinning in a circle in the center of a road that often ran rampant with logging trucks. We didn't have seat belts on, and when we ended up on the edge of the opposite bank, I was horrified to realize that we weren't yet coming to a stop.

"We're going over!" Jay yelled.

I braced myself as best I could while the truck rolled down the steep bank. We came to a jarring halt upright at the bottom of a twenty-foot drop. I was astonished to discover that my head was on the seat and my feet were braced against the ceiling. We were showered with bits of glass, and the windshield was a stunning mosaic of cracks laced with holes and held together by a thread of luck. It was the first time in my life that I had been in any kind of automobile accident, and even in my mild state of shock, I felt thankful that Nat and Ben weren't with us. Remarkably, we all escaped with minor cuts. When I stumbled back up the bank I was completely confused and couldn't tell which way was town and which way was home. The battered truck was pointing back toward town. Luckily, Mike, the same friend who loaned us the vehicle for our Suskwa Valley trip, happened along, and he took Ian back to town while we continued on our way. For hours afterwards I pulled bits of glass out of my hair and even my pockets.

Now as we approached Meziadin Junction, Nat and Ben, freshly bathed and dressed in their town clothes, grinned with enthusiasm as we turned south. In the back of the truck we hauled our ski-doo and sled for transportation into the Suskwa Valley. The road was very slick, and I held tightly onto Ben as Jay failed to negotiate the turn and instead drove us straight up a snowbank on the opposite side. As we came to a sudden stop, Natalia bumped her head on the dash. Luckily, that was the worst of the injuries, and it wasn't long before some fellows from Stewart came along and helped push us out of our predicament and we were on our way again.

We had arranged to meet Jean at the Totem Café in the town of New Hazelton, and she glided in on time in a calf-length wool skirt, her waist-length brown hair hanging loose. Her skin was pale and clear, and what struck me most about her was how peaceful she seemed. Jean Christian and Paul Glover had contacted us and visited after reading an article of mine in *Harrowsmith*. They were our nearest alternative community to the south, and they shared a similar existence and philosophy. Jean was knowledgeable about herbs and taught others about them and also conducted classes in meditation at the college in Terrace. Paul was a piano tuner by trade as well as an active environmentalist who was doing his best to save the surrounding forests from total exploitation by the timber industry. What made the association even more special was the fact that their daughter Tlell was only a year older than Natalia, and their tiny daughter Yeva was the same age as Ben. With blond curls and dark brown eyes, Tlell was beautiful. During their visit to us it soon became evident that she had the same rough-and-ready energy as Natalia, and when it came to fun wrestling, they were an even match.

Jean and Paul's home was seventeen miles off the main highway. I rode with Jean ten miles north along a winding logging road, while Jay followed in the truck with Nat and Ben. A deep blanket of snow lay across the land, and once we had parked the vehicles, we hitched the sled to the ski-doo for the remaining seven miles. In winter, when they were snowbound, the Suskwa Valley folks normally used skis to travel to and from their vehicles. Ben rode in front of Jay on the machine while Natalia, Jean, and I piled on the sled on top of our suitcase and other bundles. Natalia was very excited at the prospect of seeing Tlell, and her cheeks were bright in the winter air. As we wound our way deep into the valley, passing numerous clear-cuts in varying stages of regeneration, the ski-doo lunged smoothly over the mounds while the sled took the bumps in a less kindly manner. At the far end of one hillock, Nat, Jean, and I left the sled in unison, still hanging on to one another, and landed unscathed in a single unit in the soft snow. Jay couldn't hear us holler above the noise of the engine, and it was Ben who noticed the missing passengers. Jean had recently learned that she was three months pregnant, and we decided that it would be best to walk the remainder of the way. In about a mile we came upon Abigail Patch's farm. Abigail, or Nabby as her friends called her, was forty, and had been living in the Suskwa Valley for twenty years. Originally from Vermont, Nabby had come out to British Columbia with a partner, but when their relationship fell apart she had stayed on with her horses and goats. A spare blond woman well versed in the field of astrology, Nabby enjoyed her solitude. Next we came to the home of David and Erly, another couple who had settled in the Suskwa. Finally, at the base of a hill, was the snug home where Jean and Paul lived with their children. Jean told me that they lived in a shack and would likely always live in a shack because they had decided that what was important in this life was relationships, and they spent a good deal of time away from home nurturing their friendships. Jean still packed water from the creek in five-gallon buckets, but she told me that she didn't mind because she liked to visit the creek. I found their small, crudely finished home cozier than ours, and it was resonant with much-played musical instruments. Ben, shy and clinging to me at first, soon trotted over to touch the marimba, which sat in the center of the single room downstairs. A piano lined a west wall. It wasn't long before Ben was playing with Yeva, and for Nat and Tlell no warm-up period was necessary. They plunged into play and bounced back and forth between tumbling in the snow and talking and laughing in Tlell's room. Paul and Jean had decided not to enroll Tlell in the correspondence program and were instead educating their children free-form. Eventually Tlell chose to enter the government course because she felt a desire to learn what other girls her age were learning.

We spent four days in the Suskwa Valley, and it was a visit that I will never forget—not because we did a great deal, but because it was so satisfying to be with people with whom I felt so connected. They cared about the earth and lived consciously because of it. They practiced yoga and meditation, and sang. It was a joy to spend two hours one night singing our hearts out. It also stirred up within me a longing to have more access to people like them. And it was good for Natalia and Ben to see that we were not the only family living remotely and close to the earth.

However, such families were few and far between. Our nearest neighbors in the opposite direction who shared a similar life-style and value system were the Thunderstorms, and they lived a hundred miles north-west of us, as the crow flies, in Glenora. To drive there took about seven hours. Even though I had corresponded with the family and Jay had made one trip up with Natalia and Ben, I didn't have an opportunity to meet them until July of 1989. Jay's brother Julian was good enough to lend us his truck for this rare family outing. We left on a Sunday morning right after breakfast. Vanity prevented me from applying insect repellent to my freshly washed hair, and I suffered for it on the sultry, buggy hike out, laden with pack and a large bag of carefully selected secondhand clothes. I knew that they would have to be 100 percent cotton or wool to meet with Lynne's approval. Ben, age three and a half, hiked most of the way out, so anxious was he to make the trip to Glenora. With relief we all piled into Julian's streamlined truck and sped away, leaving most of the mosquitoes behind. What struck me as we drove north was how the landscape opened up, allowing our eyes to embrace so much more sky. One hundred twenty miles later we were in the tiny town of Dease Lake, where we hit rush hour at the Boulder Café. Natalia's and Ben's eyes almost fell out of their heads staring at all the faces in the crowded little room. Then Ben's attention fastened on a weathered and ancient Indian man with Coke-bottle glasses and a red baseball hat who smacked appreciatively after each bite of his lemon meringue pie.

From Dease Lake we headed west to Telegraph Creek. We traversed an old-time country road flanked by grassy expanses with smatterings of blood-red wild strawberries. The sky held colossal thunderheads, billowing emblems of power against a pale blue background. Gradually the growth became less and less dense until we were driving through a semi-desert zone where the colors and contours of the land elbowed through scanty vegetation. Suddenly we were confronted by signs warning of a 20 percent grade ahead. I held my breath as the descent began. The single-laned switchback road with hairpin turns, a gravel washboard surface, and not so much as a trace of a guardrail twisted down, down, down thousands of feet to the sprightly Tuya River. We crossed the river on a narrow bridge conspicuously void of railings and wound back up another series of hair-raising hairpin switchbacks to the same elevation from which we had just descended. Once on top it was too soon to relax. The road then cut along a high, narrow ridge of land flanked by the Tuya River thousands of feet below to the right and the Stikine River just as far below to the left. We were all piled into the front of the truck, and as Nat and I chewed our fingernails, I muttered that this road should be declared illegal, and that if I lived at Telegraph Creek I would never go out.

Finally we wound our way down into a valley to the minute town of Telegraph Creek. It was a curious blend of historical buildings and decaying easy-come easy-go native houses. After a stop for ice cream and fresh local strawberries at the Riversong Café, the verandah of which overlooks the powerful Stikine River, we drove the remaining fifteen miles to Glenora.

It seemed suitable to arrive at the Thunderstorm farm to the tune of loud claps of thunder. First to greet us was nine-year-old Raven, with dark eyes and hair accentuated by fair skin. She and Natalia, both craving a close friend in their lives, took to each other like moths to a light. Next Lynne came prancing barefoot down the hill to meet us. She and her husband, Nava, were both from New York originally. Lynne, a self-proclaimed feminist, organic gardener, and environmentalist, had fought long and hard to save the Stikine, one of the last free-flowing rivers, from industrial development. Nava was quiet and unassuming, with a wisdom that often went unexpressed. Their oldest daughter, eighteen-year-old Leaf, had never been to public school and had taken only a smattering of correspondence courses, but when she decided to attend college in Grande Prairie she was accepted on the strength of an interview, and she excelled at all subjects.

The Thunderstorms had built their house high on a hill with a splendid view of the Stikine River and Coast Mountains to the south, and their thriving garden and orchard—where they grew luscious strawberries, tomatoes, and even apples—and Glenora Mountain to the north.

The interior of their small house was artfully done. Expansive windows overlooked the river and mountains to the south. The solid wood furniture was brought alive with the bright array of colors in Lynne's natural-fiber rag rugs and giant cushions. Lynne had also taken great pains to make all the bedding, including vivid quilts and mattresses.

Soon Shadow Fox, a wispy two-year-old with blond hair halfway down his back and blue saucer eyes, woke up. Fox was still being breast-fed and he didn't talk much, but he did confide in me that his name was Yat. When I chatted to him he would fasten his gaze on the ground, but soon the sky-blue eyes would lift, and I'd hear a pussy-willow-soft "Hi." Fox was too young to really play with Ben, but they certainly kept track of each other.

Soon we drew out gifts of homegrown wheat, caraway, canned moose, date loaf, and used clothes. Lynne had prepared fresh bread and goat's cheese.

We had arrived at haying time, and we all pitched in with turning it in the fields and loading it onto the wagon pulled behind the tractor. Lynne and I weeded opposite each other on the same row of carrots broken by marigolds. At that time, most of Lynne's thunder was being directed against charismatic Christianity, which was spreading rapidly through the local population. One of Lynne's long-standing friendships had terminated after a fiery argument over abortion. I, who had endured a great deal of loneliness living in isolation, was reminded that even when people are available, relating to them is never simple.

Upstairs was my favorite room—the library. High windows lined the front, and the stairs came up one side. Two walls were laden with shelves holding a feast of titles, all organized into categories. I could have happily remained there for days. But we spent most of our time outside, and the temperature hovered around 80°F. Even though their homesite was beautiful, I found myself a little thirsty without a creek meandering through. The Thunderstorms used a hydraulic ram for water in summer, and during the winter they melted snow. A chute led into a large barrel located in the corner of the kitchen behind the wood cookstove.

While Lynne and I turned hay in the goat field we talked about our lives, our philosophies, our fears, and our hopes. With each subsequent visit from Lynne I felt inspired to remember my own strength as well as my rights as a human being. At the same time, Natalia and Raven were planting the first seeds of a friendship that would grow as they did. Both girls were accustomed to relating to animals, and when they were together, barefoot and wearing patched jeans, they shared each other's chickens the way some girls would share dolls. In future years, when Raven stayed overnight in the Ningunsaw Valley, I would fall asleep to whispers from the bed at the far end of the upstairs room, and when I would awake at 7:30 a.m. their bed would be empty. The two girls regularly escaped to the chicken coop at 5:30 a.m. to visit the hens together. And at Raven's home she and Nat lingered in the goat pen and rode Leaf's horse, Lalani.

We all hiked down to the Stikine River one afternoon. As soon as we arrived at the broad brown river with its spacious shores of fine black sand, Raven and Nat were out of their clothes and scampering through the water. Before long they were digging holes and burrowing into the sand like clams. While Ben, in railroad overalls, crouched close by, the girls created sand sculptures. They both giggled mischievously as Raven, half buried, shaped the sand into a pregnant belly and breasts.

Natalia and Raven also loved to dress up, and both of our households contained an abundance of costume material. Between visits Raven and Nat wrote back and forth, pouring out their rage over any injustices done to them, sharing their joys and sorrows, and exchanging dreams. Nat made many trips to Glenora, and when Raven's need for braces made monthly visits to an orthodontist in Terrace necessary, the bonus was regular overnight stays with Natalia on the way home. And I had the pleasure of seeing Lynne.

Several times Natalia and Ben traveled by bus with me to visit my family at Shuswap Lake. There they got a chance to know my family and experience the sheer pleasure of vacations at the lake. Every summer of my childhood was spent at Magna Bay, and I'll never forget the feeling of freedom scampering barefoot down the smooth dirt road, which danced with leaf shadows, and the tantalizing sparkle of the lake beyond. Into it my sister and I would plunge countless times each day. Indeed, by September our bathing suits would begin to rot because we never gave them a chance to dry out. At that time the most sophisticated watercraft we used to navigate the lake was a seaworthy log. With a smooth branch for a paddle, we'd plow through the water. Across the lake stretched peace and serenity.

My children witnessed a radically different scene. Each summer the lake was bombarded with obnoxious jet-skis, battalions of speedboats with water-skiers in tow, and hundreds of houseboats with raucous denizens. A cloud of gasoline fumes hovered above the once-pure water. Few seemed to recognize that the lake was alive and should be honored and listened to. Instead they acted as though it was there for their convenience and pleasure, and nothing further.

Despite the noise and congestion, Natalia and Ben both learned to swim at Shuswap Lake, and they loved their holidays in a region that had been home to my family for five generations. For Ben, Grandma Lorna's hard-held two acres was a paradise.

In 1990, Ben, Natalia, and I had the opportunity to travel to Vancouver with my sister Donna and her family. As the spacious car sailed down the freeway toward the main city in British Columbia, piloted by Donna's husband Rick, Nat and Ben became more sober. Ben, with his baseball cap pulled low, was standing on the seat leaning against Rick's broad shoulder. Rick, with his gentle manner, noted, "We're going to be in Vancouver pretty soon, Ben." From beneath the brim of his baseball cap, Ben carefully scrutinized one side of the flashing freeway and then the other. In a deep and serious voice Ben asked his uncle, "Which side is it on?"

Soon the city, smelling of exhaust fumes and foreign spices, was all around us. For a special treat we took the kids to Science World, a silver bubble originally built for Expo '86. Nat and Ben were fascinated with the dinosaur collection and all the hands-on displays. For a brief spell Natalia, ever independent, got lost. Her mind raced through the full gamut of scenarios and concluded that it was best to keep a sharp eye on your guardians while out in huge public complexes. When I found her she was on her way down to the main desk to turn herself in.

Science World was also the site of Omnimax, the world's largest dome screen, and we decided to take in the show. Sitting comfortably on a cliff of soft chairs, Ben was beside me as the dome darkened. Suddenly the entire theater was pulsating with extraterrestrial music. When bizarre colors began to spiral down on us, seemingly from the far reaches of the universe, Ben wailed, "I wanna go home!"

As anxious as I was to see the main feature about the history of flying, I prepared to usher my son outside. Instead he planted himself firmly in my lap and was willing to view the rest of the dazzling show from the safety of that vantage point. Back in the bush, when Ben talked about his trip to Science World, he didn't mention his terror, only the marvels of it all.

Living as remotely as we did, I considered it essential for the children to get out and see firsthand the diverse wonders of our world. Together we delighted in the joy of discovery and brought memories of shared experiences back to our little corner of the world.

Chapter 15

In Praise of Nature

N AT, NEARLY TWELVE, her shoulder-length hair drawn up in a perky ponytail, led me carefully across the straggle of dead grass through which poked raspberry canes and wild Canada mint. The air was full of the fragrance of spring as we wound our way through elderberry and gooseberry bushes, all on the verge of bursting into blossom. Our destination was a giant pair of gray-barked balsam trees that clutched a bank in a secluded bend of the creek. Wide branches, hung with old man's beard, sprawled out toward each other in an intricate maze.

"See?" Nat whispered. I craned my neck to spot the source of her joy. In the play of light and shadow on the branches, which bobbed gently in the wind, I couldn't pick out anything unusual. Then on the lowest branch hanging farthest out over the sparkling stream, I finally saw the treasure. My gaze was guided by the flash and buzz of a female rufous hummingbird. The walnut-sized hummingbird nest, attached to the branch like a burl to a birch, rocked lightly in the breeze. If it hadn't been for the flying missions of the mother bird, Natalia would never have noticed it. It was simply too tiny. For years Natalia and I had longed to see a hummingbird nest, and we exchanged a look of pure delight.

Slipping off our shoes and socks, we waded into the creek for a closer view. We were very careful not to touch it or disturb it. Cradled in the green-needled bough was the tiniest nest we had ever seen. Its symmetrical exterior held an ornate coating of leaf lichen. Inside was a pillow of delicate white cottonwood down. In the center of this softness, like heritage beans from a priceless collection, glowed two white eggs the size of navy beans.

"How long will it take?" Natalia whispered.

"About a week," I breathed.

Seven days later we peeked in the nest again and saw two featherless creatures no bigger than jelly beans. One week after that, Natalia and I were down gathering clover for rabbit food when we decided to check the nest again. Within the past few days, at Jay's invitation and to Nat's and my dismay, at least four different visitors had ventured down to see it, and we were worried that the mother may have abandoned her offspring after being disturbed too much.

Laying our sumptuous bunch of horsetails, gosling bound, upon the mint-tufted ground, we ventured over cautiously. Sitting on the balsam needle–strewn bank, we pulled off our shoes and socks, already wet from the raindrop-covered clover, tugged our jeans up to the knees, and stepped into the frigid water of the creek. As I ducked under one wide branch for a bird's-eye view, I expected the worst.

"Oh, look," Natalia sighed.

It took a moment for my eyes to comprehend the vision. Soft downy black and red feathers filled the nest, and two tiny heads were tipped up, their eyes sealed shut. Two black beaks, each no longer than a large gooseberry thorn, were rested against the rim of their cottonwood down and lichen nest world. Their breathing was marked by the rapid rise and fall of their pristine feathers. The rufous female, which we could hear buzzing around in an alder thicket on the far side of the creek, had hatched forth miniatures of the smallest bird species in the world, and seeing them at close range was a rare privilege.

Moments such as this, or the finding of a special spider or dragonfly, were enormously meaningful to Ben and Natalia. Such gifts revealed to them that the world was not static but living, breathing, and flowing, and also that there was always room for the unexpected. From the beginning, Natalia and Ben had a deep connection with nature and grew to recognize that they were part of the earth, forest, rock, water, and even air. I believe that if this bond isn't forged early in life, a later attempt to merge with nature will, at best, result in an intellectual union. Living in the bush fostered within them a deep sense of place.

In May, as the gooseberry leaves revealed their brilliant green, even Natalia—only five years old—would be caught up in her own celebration of spring. Decked out in a calf-length cotton dress and ankle socks, she would happily dance and prance about the yard and garden, a sight that always made me smile.

Toward the end of each May it was a ritual to take both children to view the *Calypso bulbosa* in bloom. The delicate purple, yellow, and white lady's slippers grew in the depths of the forest, close to the moss, and we dropped to our hands and knees to inhale the fragrance more exotic than any French perfume. The flowers, as fragile as they were exquisite, resisted transplanting, and it seemed like a miracle each spring when they reappeared and then quietly retreated into the soil again, their mysteries intact.

Summers passed all too quickly, and during this fleeting season Natalia and Ben were almost exclusively outside. Some years the weather itself provided a drama that intensified the togetherness my children and I shared. On the first of July 1989, the sky was inky black to the north and east, and I told three-year-old Ben that we had better go and pick pansies for the dinner table before it started to rain. While the small blond boy clasped my hand, we scurried down the hill and began to gather the burgundy, rose, and yellow polychrome faces beneath the distant drumrolls of thunder. I kept glancing up to see the lightning as the storm drew closer. At that time Ben was my devoted buddy, and in his deep, slow voice he told me, "I like you, Mom," at least thirty times a day. Each time I would reply, "I like you too, Ben."

Soon fat drops of rain began to strike the lush potato patch and the rest of the garden, and a sweet smell rose from the earth. The rain increased in tempo to a hissing downpour and Ben and I dashed for shelter in the wheelhouse. We stood holding hands in the open doorway and watched the most dramatic thunder and lightning storm that I had seen since childhood, and that Ben had ever seen. Each new explosion, as loud as cannons at close range, was announced by a brilliant flash of lightning.

"Here comes another one," I'd warn Ben, but he'd still jump with each new rumble and crack of thunder, which tore the ebony sky apart. The sky roared with the regularity of labor pains, giving birth to fresh torrents of rain. Within minutes the path to the dam and the wheelhouse was transformed into a river of mud and the pond was a mass of dancing drops. In three-quarters of an hour we had more rain than we'd received all the previous month.

I could feel the thunder shake the wheelhouse, and its vibrations passed through our bodies. I could tell by Ben's tense expression that he was afraid, and I too felt waves of fear pass through me. Mostly though, I reveled in the power of nature and the presence of the small boy to whom I had given birth and whose life was so entwined with mine.

The coming of autumn didn't daunt the children's spirits or their love of the outdoors. I can recall five-year-old Nat on a September morning in the yard while the frost still coated everything. Wearing mittens and a wool hat, she was collecting colored leaves in a wrinkled brown paper bag. She made a bouquet with some of them, oblivious to black spots on the smooth gold. They were all beautiful to her.

Even the wolf choruses, which wafted down the valley in any season, were chilling and also thrilling. They reminded me that the mystery of life is not a problem to be solved but a reality to be experienced.

One bird that perpetually mystified us was the water ouzel. In December of 1990, while skiing out by the river, Nat and I were surprised to see no fewer than eight of these reputedly solitary birds. We had read that this plump, stub-tailed relative of the wren was the only aquatic songbird in North America. We watched them do their rhythmic squats on shelves of ice extending precariously out over swift green water and shivered as one dove unflinchingly into the main current. In fact, we watched one make twenty consecutive dives, three to six seconds apart. They winged through the water and then walked along the bottom in search of small fish, insects, and aquatic invertebrates. Swooping low over the current, these dippers never strayed far from the water, which they worshipped in song all winter long. It was startling to hear such a lilting melody in the hushed and introverted whiteness of winter.

A few days later, the air hummed with the vibration of millions of snowflakes that had flickered down all day, piling in heaps in the garden and yard. Natalia, Ben, and I set out walking. Strange creatures had swelled up where once there was a wood stack, a seesaw, and a wheelbarrow. The snow was scattered with birch seeds, and little feathered seed eaters, including crossbills, siskins, redpolls, and juncos, pulsated as single bodies from birch clump to alder stand. While bears, woodchucks, and bats curled up in their caves for the season, the sky was vibrant with the motion of large flocks of winter birds. Their song was a welcome light in the shrinking days of winter, when the deciduous trees stand as rigid as wrought iron against the pale sky.

The fresh snow was richly embroidered with squirrel and mouse trails, which Nat guarded with a fierce backward glance, insisting that I not step on any of the minute passageways. They vanished into tiny round tunnels in the snowbanks, and Ben knelt, and closed one eye, and peered into the hidden depths. We could only imagine all the animal activity going on hidden from view. What if a mouse and a weasel bumped noses in the white maze, Nat wondered. I suspected, I told her, that the weasel, lean and wily and ever the predator, would win out over a white-footed deer mouse, the likes of whom we had discovered in the cupboard, hiding its head with its paws and trembling. We could just imagine the chatter of a squirrel chancing upon a ruffed grouse burrowed into the snow and see the explosion of bird flapping for the nearest tree, scattering the squirrel back down the tunnel.

We measured the progression of winter by the path of the sun, and in our life, which ebbed and flowed with the rhythm of the seasons, in some ways December 21 was more significant than December 25. Our souls sang in celebration of winter solstice and the passing of the shortest day of the year. Usually it was accompanied by plunging temperatures, and our breath hung like moss on the biting air. The sun was at its most elusive phase, as though it lacked the energy required to rise above the mountain peaks. Instead it skimmed the ridges, transforming trailing clouds to luminous manes. After an hour of light, when the valley was once again bathed in optimism, the sun spun behind South Mountain, not emerging from the far side until the late afternoon. After twenty minutes it sank without resistance behind the spires of tall spruce. When Ben was three he told me that the sun is love, and I wondered about living in a land where it eluded us for days on end, even in summer. A loss of direct sunlight can sometimes signal a loss of hope.

At other times the northern sky made us all believe in miracles. It came alive with dancing displays of the aurora borealis. In March 1988, we witnessed the most spectacular northern lights that I had ever seen. Up until then I had never viewed them in any color other than moonstone. What caught our attention at ten that evening was the rosy glow in the east. If it had been summer, we would have thought that the ridge was on fire, but since our valley was still snowbound, we knew otherwise. We stood on the porch awestruck by a sky throbbing with color. A skirt of cloud, in all hues of the prism, gathered at the highest point at the center of the sky and cascaded down the entire nightscape. Then as the top of the cloud-skirt expanded, we stood beneath a funnel of shimmering red, green, yellow, and mauve lights that seemed to stretch up to eternity. The aurora borealis pulsated and swirled about the sky like colored chiffon skirts adorned with gemlike stars. Then we watched in wonder as two wing-shaped clouds entered from the sides of the funnel, joined together, and flew at high speed up the night sky, up the cone of light, until they vanished from sight through the apex. It was a scene that I will never forget, a vivid reminder of our own smallness.

Living in the wilderness was a supreme lesson in humility for our children as well as for me. When we saw the conditions under which other citizens of the valley survived, and even flourished, it struck a deep chord within us. Such intimacy with the natural world bred a deep respect. Living close to the earth, Natalia and Ben appreciated the worth of every living creature, every species of flora and fauna. My children sensed that they themselves were only one small part of a multifaceted, mysterious, and holy realm called Nature.

Sadly, we realized that this reverence for all life was not universal. Up until 1985, there was no logging to speak of north of Meziadin Junction, ninety miles to the south. But in just two short years, logging companies, like an army on the move, destroyed thousands of acres of timber, creating what would turn out to be one of the largest clear-cuts in British Columbia. In the process, they had cut access roads into valleys and regions that had never been visited by humans before. The Stewart-Cassiar Highway itself was turned largely into a haul road for a huge and desperate tree-liquidating operation. In 1987, as many as 350 trucks a day were dumping their loads in Stewart. This added up to about forty-two thousand truckloads a year. To make matters worse, the entire Cassiar timber supply area was allocated for wholesale log export by the British Columbia cabinet. Boats from China, Korea, and Japan picked up the logs in the port of Stewart, thus depriving many Canadians of processing jobs.

Mile after mile along the Stewart-Cassiar Highway this desolate scene of adjacent clear-cuts repeated itself, and we dreaded its advancement north. After all, we had come to know the trees as individuals—the cottonwood with the woodchuck spyhole, the balsam that a bear had carved with sharp claws, the pine beside Desiré Lake that I had focused on while I waited for Natalia to be born. Natalia and I waged our own battle for the preservation of two scarred birch that Jay wanted to fell on the hill near the house. It was his wish to open up the view more, but my daughter and I felt that our realm would be a little poorer without their presence. We won that battle, and red-breasted sapsuckers still stutter bugs from their bark while squirrels skitter up and down them. The thought of whole forests that I knew and loved so well falling filled me with despair.

Although for months there were rumors that timber sales were going to be put up for bid on a large bench of virgin land above our valley home, we came across the first real indicators in the fall of 1988 while walking the trail that threaded its way northwest to Desiré Lake. We were stopped in our tracks by the sight of gaudy plastic ribbons hung on branches and draped across the trail. Patches of outer bark had been stripped off some of the trees and the inner bark had been blasted with blood-red spray paint. Black numbers were tattooed into their sides. Until now, we had been the only beings, apart from the bears, wolves, and moose, who used this trail regularly. What sickened me most was that when other humans had ventured through this boreal forest, they did so in order to destroy it.

Natalia's face registered rage as she reached up and ripped an orange ribbon from a lean pine. I also vented my anger by yanking some of the death tags off the trunks and branches. However, we soon realized that the ribbons went for miles and miles, their gay colors contrasting sharply with their dark purpose. Even though we vowed to stop the loggers, we knew that with any act of sabotage we would simply be cutting our own throats. We were the only residents for miles around, and all fingers would point at us.

A full year later, in the fall of 1989, I climbed the hill and began to hike in the direction of Desiré Lake. The air smelled like snow as I wound my way through the boreal forest, noticing two porcelain mushrooms growing out of the side of a cottonwood and brown devil's club leaves as limp as wet handkerchiefs. To the north I saw what had become a sadly familiar excess of sky. The clear-cut, only a stone's throw away, made me feel stripped of my leaves, unprotected from the wheels of destruction. A melancholy air hung about the trees flanking the clear-cut, as though shocked into silence by the violence they had witnessed.

Only minutes later I fought and tripped my way over several sturdy spruce that had fallen directly across our trail. Still, I didn't get the biggest jolt until I reached my favorite spot halfway between Desiré Lake and the valley. There a natural moss and lichen garden capped a rocky outcrop that overlooked a bowl of wooded land. In the distance stood the gleaming peaks of the Coast Mountains. Regularly, we stopped there with the children to drink in the breeze and the view. An intricacy of gnarled pines graced the knoll where we would go to pick lowbush cranberries and saskatoons.

That day I suddenly found myself ejected from the safety of the woods into a scene that was so unfamiliar it was disorienting. The pristine pine forest was gone. Every tree to the north had been toppled; I could see the base of the lookout ridge two miles away. A strong odor rose from the mass of fallen trees from which jutted broken limbs, chewed-up trunks. The very earth was stripped of its moss by the passing of the Goliath equipment. As I stood dazed by the magnitude of the destruction, Shakespeare's words ran through my mind: "Pardon me thou bleeding piece of earth that I am meek and gentle with these butchers."

In what was formerly an easily traversed stretch of woods, I now found myself struggling through the tangle of fallen trees in an attempt to get to our resting spot. My path was blocked in every direction, and I sank to a spruce log. There was such a facelessness to it all! The loggers were strangers who invaded, conquered the forest, and roared away without so much as a backward glance, leaving us and the animals with a wasteland and their garbage. They were simply doing jobs. Did they not see how our souls shrank a little with each falling tree? As a member of the human race I knew that I was partly responsible. Yet I recognized that we are as dependent on nature as a fetus is on its mother. As we mutilate the earth we mutilate ourselves.

I thought that I was alone until I saw, less than two feet away on another log, a red squirrel holding a cone and studying me. It looked as lost as any refugee, and I thought of the multitude of animals, both large and small, that would not survive this assault on their home.

We had always felt safe in our own home until August 5, 1990. The day even began on a strange note. Ben came in to tell me that Schwarzy, the rabbit doe, had given birth to a headless baby. Later, when Jay was hiking out with a load of potatoes for a truck driver who had given him a ride, he met two surveyors coming through the trees.

On June 15 of the same year we had learned that the $20 million Iskut Road, expected to cross the Ningunsaw River to the south of us, had been given the go-ahead by the British Columbia cabinet. Oddly, the environmental studies were expected to be done after approval had already been granted. Suddenly we found ourselves living just east of what was being referred to as "the golden triangle," one of the most mineral-rich areas in western Canada. The road would give access to the mineral-laden Iskut Valley and open the area up to development, which would ultimately destroy the existing wilderness. We mourned that in the midst of a multifaceted environmental crisis clutching the entire planet, this type of exploitation could be heralded as progress.

The surveyors were friendly enough, and they asked Jay where he was headed. When he explained that he was bringing his potatoes to a trucker, they appeared baffled. One asked, "Potatoes from where?"

"Down in the valley there," Jay answered, motioning with his hand.

The two men's faces registered genuine shock. They had no idea that anyone lived in the Ningunsaw region. It turned out that a consulting firm from Vancouver had done an expensive and "thorough" study for the government. Now it was the job of three crews of surveyors to ribbon out the entire length of the Iskut Road on foot. Their chosen route for the $20 million road ran straight down Natty Creek and directly through the center of our house! It then traversed our garden and the river flat. Ironically, ours was the only permanent house for one hundred miles in most directions. Jay drove with the surveyors, a father and son team named Stan and Kevin Brooks, down to Bell II, thirty miles south, for lunch, and Jay did his best to convince them that following the creek was not the best route.

The next morning, while young siskins flitted through the ripening grain and Natalia and Ben fed the rabbits, Jay sat by the wood cook-stove, where our own wheat cereal bubbled. With a magnifying glass and pencil, he traced in other possible routes. We were expecting the surveyors the next day.

It was a cloudy morning, and I was in the garden weeding the lilies when the surveyors arrived. With dirty hands and frayed coat cuffs, I hurried up to the house where the surveyors were inspecting maps with Jay while Nat and Ben looked on. I shook hands with them and then raced upstairs and snatched my little stack of nationally published articles. Rushing back downstairs and handing them the issues, I noted that it was odd that the well-funded Thurber Consultants had been oblivious to our presence when there were people all across the country who were aware of it. Their embarrassment intensified when, with trepidation, I vowed to put my body on the line in defense of our home if I had to. I stressed how much I would hate to see a road go in at all. To my surprise they sympathized. Natalia and Ben stayed with me while Jay led the two men upstream to look around. Later Stan confessed that he couldn't offer us much reassurance.

For three consecutive nights I lay awake imagining bizarre scenes like having to cross a road to get from the living room to the kitchen. Jay, the perennial optimist of the family, pointed out that we could always rebuild. And think of how easy it would be to sell vegetables. We would have customers coming right through our doors.

Finally, after what seemed like an eternity, we got word by radio-phone from Stan telling us that the likeliest route would be at least two miles downstream. A wave of relief washed over the valley.

Several Sundays later, Natalia and I set out to hike the alternative route that the surveyors had ribboned out through the dense woods to the west. Nat wore jeans and a turquoise kangaroo top, and I carried a pack containing lunch. It was our objective to experience the forest between the outflow from Desiré Lake and the Iskut River before the road reduced it to a dust-laden backdrop for industry. We dreaded the roar of trucks, which would rip the music of nature to shreds, send the animals fleeing, and cause chaos in the delicate natural balance. It was with mixed emotions that we toiled along the trail that wound across the river flat, while the sun ignited the sprinkling of fresh snow on the Coast Mountain peaks. The air, succulent from the rain that had fallen during the night, was sweet enough to drink. Soon dripping devil's club and thimbleberry leaves had soaked our pants, and we hurried toward the sidehill where the sun lit the birch trees like golden lamps. Natalia bounced with energy, a hawk careened overhead, and I breathed in the beauty of this place to which my soul had fastened itself.

Soon we descended to the green and galloping Ningunsaw River, which braided its strands across shifting alluvial sands. Hoping to wade across a shallow channel to gain access to the bank we had to follow, I stepped into the clear water and felt the bottom give way. In a split second I was submerged thigh high.

"Quicksand!" Nat yelled.

Grasping for more solid ground, I yanked my legs from the tugging muck. Scrambling onto the shore I shakily emptied the liquid sand from each gum boot.

"I'm sure glad Ben didn't do that," I gasped. "He would have disappeared altogether."

"Mmmm. That's for sure," Nat replied in an unconvincing tone.

Choosing another route to the bank, we then spent at least two hours maneuvering our way west along an awkward sidehill, weaving over and under windfalls, and battling with the rosebushes that snatched at our hair. Often they were the only shrub to grasp to save us from a slide to the river below, and Natalia squawked each time a thorn drove itself into her tender fingertips.

When we descended to the river flat again, Nat stopped cold and spun around with huge, frightened eyes. I looked down. Crossing a pool and coming our way over damp black sand were mammoth and deeply embedded grizzly tracks. The sight of them made us feel very small, and for a moment we wished we were back within the thick walls of our log home. At the same time I was glad of this affirmation that the land still belonged to the wild creatures—for a little while longer.

Past a tangle of alder near a narrow spot in the river, we found the *Zodiac*, a boat belonging to the survey crew, who used it for access to the opposite shore. Although I knew that a boat had once ventured down the river, it was the first that I had actually seen, and the plump gray thing, so impervious to the whims of nature, looked incongruous. Close by were sandwich wrappers, a cigarette package, and other signs of human passage. Nat groaned at the sight of them. For her entire life her family and the local animals had been the only ones who traveled the river regularly, and she had been taught not to litter.

We plunked down on a log for a rest. As we bit into our oatmeal cookies, a helicopter was suddenly hovering above us like a crazed egg-beater. We didn't recognize the two men on board, and they stared down at us, mystified as to where two humans, particularly females, had materialized from. We stared back. They darted a short distance downstream to land. Rather than wait and talk to the men and explain that we were out enjoying our backyard—a place to which they ventured only because they were being paid to do so—on an impulse we opted for vanishing into the woods. Let them wonder, we thought.

The gaudy survey ribbons now lured us northwest through a rich boreal landscape. Reveling in the sight of autumn's golden-crowned birch trees, we found it painful to ponder the coming Iskut Road. It would be built so that rich outside mining interests could gouge the mountains for their gold. Leaving them barren and scarred, a handful of humans would grow wealthy while the earth and most of its citizens grew more impoverished. Furthermore, once access was made, the logging companies would move in to skin the lower Iskut River of its old-growth forest. The complex ecosystem that my daughter and I crept through was, as yet, vibrant with life. The forest floor held a wealth of rotting wood, mosses, and mushrooms, while the upper canopy possessed leaves of the finest lace against a turquoise sky. Silver streams cascaded over ancient rock. As a chopper blasted by, a tiny red squirrel frantically scolded it. Spiders trembled in their webs. When the silence returned, it was easy to lose oneself in the microcosm of life established on an upturned tree root system.

"That might be an old bear den," Nat suggested, eyeing a hole at the base of an adjacent spruce. Nodding, I flashed on an incident of the previous winter. Loggers with their giant equipment had rooted a black bear out of its den on a bench of land above our home. They didn't even know it until its lifeless body came out with a load of logs.

Now as we studied the unearthed root system, I mused over how vital old-growth forests are, not only for their genetic code but also because about one-third of a tree's useful life occurs after it is dead. The place between the bottom of a fallen tree and the soil is one of the richest areas of the forest in terms of nutrient exchange. They also provide habitat for the little mammals that spread the spores of the vital mycorrhizal fungus. This fungus is essential to the survival of all conifers. In fact, a large, decaying fallen tree has twice the number of living cells found in a live tree. Despite their role, old-growth forests are being annihilated at an appalling rate.

After trudging a wide circuit through the dense woods, Natalia and I found ourselves at the creek that flowed out of Desiré Lake. After crossing a log spanning the small stream, we continued on through the pine and birch forest until we saw through the trees to the east a foreboding amount of sky. Beneath it sprawled a new clear-cut scattered with massive mounds of rejected logs and limbs. It was but one wee corner of a network of cut-blocks that had been cut the previous winter. Thirty-five hundred loads were hauled out of the Bob Quinn Lake area alone.

"It's so ugly," Nat complained, yanking her hood up, as though to shield herself from the devastation.

To be sure, the case against clear-cutting reaches far beyond aesthetics. It is, in essence, three-stage destruction. Cutting is followed by slash-burning, which is followed by the application of chemicals. I have seen areas where over half of what was cut was wasted. Slash-burning gets rid of any evidence of this; it also destroys the topsoil and contributes to the greenhouse effect by pumping huge quantities of carbon dioxide into the atmosphere. Next the so-called weed trees are chemically eliminated. These weed trees, which include the alder with its nitrogen-fixing nodules on its roots, are soil builders. They live out their relatively short life spans and prepare the way for another vibrant forest. Without the natural decomposition stage, the second growth is invariably inferior, and this fate is assured by the replanting of a monoculture, or the planting of only one tree species. According to Chris Maser, a private consultant in sustainable forestry and the author of *The Redesigned Forest*, with the complex diversity gone, no tree plantations have survived beyond the third rotation. Ultimately an entire ecosystem—fragile to begin with due to its northern location—is permanently destroyed.

Around Desiré Lake a mere hedge of trees had been spared—a veil of deception. We retreated, stunned, into this narrow band of living, breathing woods, but we still had a clear view of the wasteland. Except for the occasional distant roar from a skidder, the clear-cut was silent. Stagnant puddles floated oil and oil jugs. Plastic tarps, beer cans, and flagging ribbon were strewn about the ruins of what only months earlier had been a vibrant virgin forest.

I was well aware that there were those who questioned our right to live in the wilderness. But our clearing had changed little in a decade, and we tried to give back to the land by gardening organically and by caring deeply about the land. I was confident that after we were gone the small scar we inflicted upon the earth would heal. Conversely, in a matter of weeks, industry, in the name of progress and short-term profit, could destroy thousands of acres of ancient forest—truly a crime against nature.

Following the shoreline through the pine and bunchberry, we noticed that even the veil of deception had been violated. Someone had cut a swath, making it possible to drive right to the water's edge. Wearily we slogged on toward the north end of the lake and finally came to a stop in front of the octagonal cabin. A weathered bear that Jay had carved long ago still sat outside, and some chimes tinkled vacantly in the breeze from the lake. Turning toward the lake, we walked to the edge and felt the water. Frigid, as always. Scanning the surface, I knew that this place would always be sacred to me. After all, it was the place where I had given birth to Natalia, while the loons celebrated her arrival with joyous laughter. Today the loons were nowhere in sight.

As the wind rose, the birch trees bordering the lake trembled, releasing a rain of golden leaves upon Desiré Lake. Turning north, Natalia and I hiked the mossy ridge trail that had first led me to Jay's cabin over a decade earlier. I recalled the wildland that had flowed uninterrupted in every direction. Just short of Bob Quinn Lake we were stopped abruptly by the sight of something alien. The quiet hollow where I had come to gather kinnikinnick when I was pregnant with Natty was spanned by a dry, brown, culvert-clutching monstrosity. In a matter of three weeks a new logging road, branching off the Iskut Road, had invaded this quiet corner, and more timber sales loomed on the horizon.

As Natalia, with her fair skin and truth-demanding eyes, flopped on the shore for a rest, I tried to read her expression. I was raising my children with the belief that all life was sacred. How could she possibly incorporate the magnitude and senselessness of the destruction she had witnessed into this philosophy? Natalia didn't speak, but her face seemed to ask, how could anyone pass a death sentence on such beauty? After all, we are the earth. Our bodies are largely water. When we cry, we cry the ocean.

Living close to the earth provided Ben and Natalia with a good beginning. Sooner or later they will venture forth to explore the world. I expect that they will both spend most of their years in a rural setting, but I can't say this for sure. As evolving souls we follow our own life path. We can only guide our children. We can't walk the path for them. Rather than asking if our children will remain in the wilderness, a more crucial question haunts me. Will any wilderness remain for our children?

Epilogue

THE SUMMER OF 1992 was the worst summer of my life. Jay wanted to take Natalia and Ben with him on a much-needed six-week vacation to Wisconsin, and I gave my consent. What I hadn't anticipated was the letter he would leave me, which stated, in essence, that he didn't wish to be married to me anymore.

Ever since I met Jay I had been in awe of his energy, talent, and abilities, and I loved him a great deal. But for many years I had been aware that our marriage was in trouble. What bothered me most was Jay's blatant disregard for my feelings, and his lack of appreciation of my efforts, which in his estimation never exceeded mediocrity. I rarely felt empowered or even validated by him, and Jay seemed to place no value on the more feminine tendency toward compassion, which took the form of loving, listening, and nurturing. But I had learned that there was no arguing with Jay, and that if I tried, he would shout me down.

Nothing puts more of a strain on a couple than living in isolation. Nonstop togetherness, despite all its positive points, can also cause a great deal of stress, and it is easy to develop a pattern of blaming each other for everything. There is also the tendency to depend on each other to fulfill every social need, and this is unrealistic. It is easy at times to lose perspective, and isolation magnifies every habit, choice, and gesture.

I was presented with the letter the day before my family left, and the next morning as I tightly hugged Nat and Ben I was in a state of shock. There I was with six weeks of solitude and a book to write, and suddenly my whole life had exploded around me. Sleep was impossible. I lay hanging on to the edges of the bed, which seemed to be spinning. My eyes were wide open, staring at the room that scarcely dimmed in the unrelenting brightness of northern summer nights, while my mind struggled to understand.

For thirteen years I hadn't really imagined life beyond the Ningunsaw Valley. I had found the home for which I had searched so long, and my roots had sunk deep into the soil. Our life-style embodied all the values I had struggled to find, and I wanted nothing more or less. It was a slow torture to remain there going through the motions of gathering clover for the rabbits, feeding the geese and chickens, shaking the blossoming tomatoes so that they would yield a good crop, lugging water in buckets up the steep slope to the attached greenhouse, weeding the garden, caring for it all, and knowing that I had to leave it. I felt at first like there was an open wound running from my throat to the base of my belly, a wound caused by my severance from the place I loved so dearly. It was as though a huge chunk of me was being torn away. Each time I stepped out onto the front porch and took in the clearing, the forest, and the mountains, my heart broke a little more. Slowly I said good-bye to the valley, the home, and the man.

As the weeks passed by I was continually overwhelmed by surges of fear, sadness, anger, shame, anxiety, and guilt, but I came to understand that real strength doesn't mean being strong all the time. Real strength comes with accepting one's feelings no matter what they may be and allowing them to come and go as they will.

The white flower season of Solomon's seal, yarrow, elderberry, and cranberry blossoms slowly turned into pink and mauve. First the wild roses flared and then the fireweed unfurled, lending a magenta blush to our clearing. As I went about my chores, I kept moving through different stages of grief, at the same time praying that Jay would have a change of heart so that we could continue what was, in so many ways, a wonderful life. I hoped that my departure would jolt him into realizing how important his family was and into making the changes necessary to create a healthier marriage.

Even though it was *our* home, because of his anger and hostility toward me, I knew that it would not be wise for me to stay. I experienced regular surges of anger over the injustice of it all. Thirteen years of my life had gone into this wilderness home as well, yet I was to be cast out of Eden into a state of poverty in a civilization that had become both alien and undesirable to me. And yet, if I could have my children, I would be taking the best of it with me. I took steps to ensure that we would be together.

What did I learn from thirteen years in the wilderness? Most of the insight will wait for the right moment to reveal itself. Consciously I learned patience, perseverance, humility, reverence, a deep sense of my own purpose, and a greater capacity to love. I discovered that I am most at peace in wildland. Above all I learned to trust in the depths of my own being, and through it the powers of the universe. I connected with the divine power—call it what you will—in a more profound way than ever before. I understood that ultimately this divine power is all there is. Love is all there is. I don't need a church to tell me this is so. For me this truth is rooted in the natural world.

As the lonely summer wore on, I came to realize that I am, in some sense, the valley now. I have absorbed enough of its beauty, rhythm, and wisdom to carry it with me. It has become part of my inner landscape, and it will sing in my blood and echo in my dreams.

Toward the end of July, I was feeling grateful that even though I was going through a crisis internally, at least externally the farm was still hanging together. One morning I sleepily arose and, as was my ritual, padded over to the window to see what kind of day it was. It had rained during the night, but the sky was calm and blue. Peering down at the garden I could scarcely believe my eyes. Ripping through the center of it lengthwise was a great torrent of brown water, which was submerging the vegetables in its path and engulfing the greenhouse! In a state of panic I tore downstairs and out into the front yard to check the dam. I'll never forget the gutted sensation I felt gazing down at the pond and seeing no pond. It had vanished completely, and what was left behind filled me with terror. It was a shallow crater of supersaturated sand—muck—with a furious flow of dirty water embracing the exposed brush island and racing for the fifteen-foot-wide rupture that it had already chewed out of the center of the dam. It was as if my whole life had unexpectedly burst apart and was surging forth to an unknown destination.

The rain that had fallen during the night was not enough to cause this destruction, and it was evident that the water level had risen at least two feet in a matter of minutes. Whole logs had been lifted out of the pond while stout chunks of cottonwood and spruce were strewn right across the garden.

With the radiophone I summoned the help of our good friends Darrell, Norma Jean, and Denis, and even though at first it looked like a hopeless task, with a huge effort we had the hole in the dam blocked within two days. Most of the repair work lay ahead. Denis hauled dirt for several days, and I was grateful for his efforts because I didn't want Jay coming home to a disaster. Denis estimated that at least three beaver dams must have broken simultaneously upstream to produce what was like a little tidal wave. It was a small reminder of how fragile our existence is.

Little did I suspect when I began this book that my wilderness life, as I had known it, would end with it. When Jay returned in August with Natalia and Ben, I met him at the Terrace airport and the kids and I traveled south to Shuswap Lake.

We are in transition now, biding our time, dealing with the huge task of adjusting to civilization. The Ningunsaw Valley will never belong to us, but we know in our hearts that we belong to it. Deep down we all want to go home.